MOTHER TO THE MOTHERLESS

MOTHER
to the
MOTHERLESS

The Inspiring Story of One Woman's Devotion to the
Orphaned Children of Kenya

MAMA ZIPPORAH

hatherleigh
Improve your life. Change your world.

Improve your life. Change your world.

Hatherleigh Press is committed to preserving and protecting the natural resources of the earth. Environmentally responsible and sustainable practices are embraced within the company's mission statement.

Visit us at www.hatherleighpress.com and register online for free offers, discounts, special events, and more.

Mother to the Motherless
Copyright © 2014 Mama Zipporah

Library of Congress Cataloging-in-Publication Data is available upon request.
ISBN: 978-1-57826-493-3

All rights reserved. No part of this book may be reproduced, stored in a retrieval system, or transmitted, in any form or by any means, electronic or otherwise, without written permission from the publisher.

Cover Design by Carolyn Kasper
Interior Design by Cynthia Dunne

Printed in the United States

10 9 8 7 6 5 4 3 2 1

CONTENTS

INTRODUCTION

꿈
꿈꿈
꿈꿈

"If you do not stand firm in your faith, you will not stand at all."
—Isaiah 7:9

I MAGINE RECEIVING DIVINE insight from God. Imagine witnessing miraculous healings that defy scientific explanation, or discovering that torch-bearing angels protect your family throughout the night. Imagine feeding hundreds daily without a penny to your name, or simply having your unspoken needs met daily by God. These are all blessings that I have experienced throughout my life of faith. Even during times of great persecution, I have stood firm in my faith. Through my experiences, I have come to personally understand the truth behind Isaiah 7:9: "If you do not stand firm in your faith, you will not stand at all."

God has blessed me with a great compassion for abused and abandoned children, and has placed a strong burden on my heart to become a voice for those too young to represent themselves. Throughout my childhood, God protected and upheld me, calling me to become something greater than anything my family could have imagined—a mother to the motherless. Now, even people I do not know greet me by shouting "Mama Zipporah!" I am honored that God would choose to work through me.

My vision of a home built specifically to tend to orphaned children in Kenya was in truth a vision from God. It was because of His call that I began The Huruma Children's Home. Developing an environment that would allow these children to grow up in a solid Christian family has become my life's purpose. And since the day my husband Isaac and I opened the doors of our small mud hut in August of 1990, God has done nothing but bless our ministry and provide for our needs, protecting us and even blessing us with his miracles. The growth and blessings that I and my children have received are not the result of any efforts I have made. Rather, it is the work of the Lord which has caused our ministry to prosper. And, to honor the mighty work which He has done, I wish to make His glory known throughout the nations.

> *"Give thanks to the Lord, call on his name; make known among the nations what he has done. Sing to him, sing praise to him; tell of all his wonderful acts."* —Psalm 105:1

Contained within this book you will find my life story. I do not share this story to bring glory upon myself; rather it is to make known the glory of our Lord and Father. Without Him, my testimony would be meaningless. As it is written in Matthew 5:16, "Let your light shine before men, that they may see your good deeds and praise your Father in heaven." I am blessed that God has chosen me, an uneducated woman, to perform such wonders through Him.

This book, my testimony, is dedicated to His glory. May all praise and honor be unto Him. I also dedicate this book to my late husband, Pastor Isaac Kamau, and my children, Caroline Naiserian, Catherine Sialo Butt, and George Layian for supporting and believing in what God called me to do. With their help, and the help of many others, I have been able to bring motherless children into our family, give them a home, and share the little we have with them.

Thank you, Lord.

—Mama Zipporah
Executive Director, Huruma Childrens Home

FAITH IN THE DARK

T HE POWER HAS gone out. It would seem as though the power company has no respect for those in the midst of worship. The sun has already tucked itself behind the Ngong Hills, and the room is filled with the gentle light of the moon as it makes its way through the open windows. It is Wednesday, the customary time for the children of Huruma to share in their evening fellowship of praise and worship, testimonies and speaking.

But without electricity, the keyboard no longer plays; the microphone is unable to project a voice. You are barely able to decipher the silhouettes of bodies surrounding you.

Yet why should something as insignificant as electrical power put an end to fellowship? Were we not able to praise God long before what's-his-name discovered electrical current? But with nearly 150 of us packed into the small church, no one was quite sure what would happen next. If everyone were to exit at once, someone was likely to be trampled upon in the dark.

Before I knew it, someone had grabbed a drum and began to pound out a rhythm. Next, one of the home's older children began to sing in a voice comparable to that of an angel. Before I knew it I was surrounded by children dancing and singing in the dark. They sang not to please anyone, nor was their dance meant to impress the ones standing beside them; we could only see the shadows of movement.

1

This harmonious movement was for God. They danced in sincerest gratitude for the blessings in their lives. Despite the darkness within the small tin church, the orphaned children praised God in a moving display of heartfelt affection. They had no audience on Earth; it was all between them and the Lord. This was worship in its truest form.

These precious dancing silhouettes have been given to my care, and I look upon them with the pride of a mother. My life has come a long way and much has been accomplished, but none of it was because of me.

✻✻✻✻✻✻

I was born, one quiet night in January of 1957, in a place called Githunguri. Outcasts of Nairobi City in Kenya, my parents Peter Kamunge Kimani and Unice Wanjiru welcomed me as their first daughter. But this welcome was not without resentment, as my father very much wanted a boy. They had already had twins before me: Kimani and Mbuiya were born in 1954, but unfortunately, they had both died when they were only two years old. In those days, most parents did not strategically plan or space out their children, as is the custom today. It was normal to give birth to children every year, which often resulted in a very large family—in our case, three boys and two girls—within a very short span of time. The seemingly large gap between my late siblings' birth and mine was not intended, either; rather, it was dictated by the prevalence of political destabilization happening at the time in our country.

Around that time, the Colonial Government had declared a state of emergency. Kenyans were restless, and growing increasingly discontented with colonial rule; they wanted to govern themselves. The Colonial Government was neither willing nor prepared to hand power back over to the Kenyans, which resulted in a struggle for freedom.

From a young age, God began preparing me for the future He had in store for me. I went through many hard times, and though I know now that the pains of my childhood were preparing me for my future ministry, at the time they seemed to go on with no end in sight.

"If at all you serve God, tell that God of yours to stop me from throwing these beans into the field!" These were my father's words, spoken in harsh anger only moments before he threw my mother's beans—and with it our family's livelihood—into the neighboring field. As my eyes filled with tears, watching the beans scatter through the air and disperse along the ground, I reflected upon the hard labor my mother had gone through to earn them. It had taken her a considerable amount of time to gather those beans for sale—they were all we had. I continued to think this, as I watched my father proceed to beat my mother. As a child, my normal tendency was to come between my father and mother at times like these, in an attempt to rescue her from the beating. I had very little fear, but my father's temper was wild and uncontrollable; this time even I feared what he might do. And so I stood there and watched as my mother collapsed to the ground. It was not until I saw my father storm off that I let out a sigh of relief.

I was nine years old.

Many psychologists believe that memory recollection can be suppressed when one experiences traumatic events. If this is true, then perhaps it was the pain of my childhood that has caused the repression of my past. In any case, this is my earliest memory from childhood. Sometimes I find myself wishing that this, too, could become just another suppressed memory, but unfortunately I can recall the event in vivid detail.

My father was a large man—in stature and in status—and was well known for his temper. I can still hear him, crying out in rage. His anger was only heightened when my mother became a Christian. But despite my father's persecution, she still awoke every morning, singing praises to God. I remember with fondness the mornings I watched her labor away at the monotonous daily tasks of the household. She never grumbled, never complained. Rather she looked at it as an opportunity to bring praises to her Lord. In a soft sweet voice, she would sing hymns of worship while hunched over, sweeping the ground with twigs she had previously collected. She would pray in gratitude to the Lord as she prepared what little food we had for breakfast. Through it all, and despite my father's abuse, she held strong to her faith, continued to go to church, and raised her family in the knowledge of God's Word.

I credit my faith in the Lord to the example my mother set. My mother's life was that of a Christian hero. She was not a famous hero; her life has not been shared with the world as a testimony to God. But all the same, she was part of the unknown army of the Lord: an army of believers scattered throughout the world, giving each day to God. Each of their individual testimonies is unique, but they all have one thing in common: insurmountable faith in God. Their accomplishments go untold and unrecognized here on Earth, but it is these quiet heroes who await their reward in Heaven. Each faces daily struggles and persecutions, yet stands strong.

My mother was one of these unknown heroes. But while she was heroic in her faith, my mother's perseverance only increased my father's fits of anger. It would have been easy for her to hide

FAITH IN THE DARK

her convictions and falsely denounce her faith. But she never did. Through beating after beating, she continued to cling to her relationship with God; never once did she deny her beliefs. My mother's faith and perseverance infuriated my father. He could never understand the motivation behind her faith, and sadly, he caused her much pain simply because she loved the Lord.

My father's temper was not something to be taken lightly, and my siblings and I were raised in an environment of great fear. The temper within him also brought on harsh, irrational behavior, so that we never knew what to expect. The bean incident was just one of many occasions in which he abused my mother in the midst of unjustified rage.

> *"So then, those who suffer according to God's will should commit themselves to their faithful Creator and continue to do good."* —1 Peter 4:19

But despite horrific abuse and persecution, my mother stood strong in her faith and inspired me to do the same. My mother's faith never wavered, no matter how dreadful the abuse she faced. I am proud to say that by the age of nine, my mother had taught me how to read the Bible, and on December 18, 1966, I accepted the Lord as my personal savior and was baptized within my mother's church. For my mother, this was a proud moment; unfortunately, it caused great tension between my father and me. In an instant my relationship with him was changed. My baptism created a wide distance between the two of us. I was now, like my mother, the one he detested most.

MY MOTHER, MY HERO

Y MOTHER WAS the first woman my father took as a
bride, in 1953. However, after he was employed by the
Ministry of Environment, Water and Natural Resources as a forest ranger, my father began to attract the attention of many other
women aside from my mother. In Kenya, it is extremely common for a man to have multiple wives. In fact, there are some
men who believe it is their right to take more wives than there
are days of the week. I do not understand how one man can
hope to uphold his marital responsibilities when he has multiple
families to provide for; it is not possible. In any event, my father
certainly could not.

But having multiple wives or taking on a mistress was far too
closely associated with status and power; it comes with bragging
rights among most male groups. My father was seen as a wealthy
and persuasive man within our community. Individuals interested
in purchasing land from him would, in addition to money, frequently offer a young woman to entice his interest and secure
the sale. Over time, my father accumulated many mistresses in
this way. And each one was better provided for than his true
family. I grew up with the understanding that my father cared
more for them than he did for us. Were it not for the support we
received through my mother's church, I am not sure how our
family would have survived.

We had many financial struggles, which the church helped to pay for, including our education, which was a cost that the family could not have afforded otherwise. There were six of us, not counting my father, all squeezed into that cramped little shack in a small village in the forest. I remember returning home each night from school to a dark, empty house. One might have thought that our little shack had been robbed, but it hadn't; we had so little that there was no reason for a robber to enter our home. We were often unable to afford paraffin oil to light the lamp. So, with our unsatisfied stomachs growling in despair, we would squat around the fire pit, hoping to use what little light it offered in a hopeless attempt to complete our homework. Occasionally we would get too close to the fire and singe the corners of our workbooks, but we had no other options.

I grew to despise poverty. As a young child, I could not fathom how an individual could be left with nothing, while others, such as my father, lived a comfortable life far above destitution and nearing gluttony. Influenced greatly by biblical Sunday school teachings, I decided that I would not become like my father. I was not going to simply accept poverty as an unchangeable aspect of society; rather, I was going to help those less fortunate.

My dislike of poverty grew to such heights that at the age of nine, in my childish logic, I vowed never to marry a man who owned a donkey. There was no true logical reasoning behind my dislike of donkeys—it is not as though I was ever harmed by one—but I associated donkeys with poverty. In my immature reasoning I vowed to never marry a man from the nearby rift-valley, simply because it was an area of many donkeys. I believed (far too naively as it turned out) that this would keep me from living a life of poverty and allow me to help those less fortunate.

A FLEETING GLIMPSE OF JOY

THROUGHOUT MY CHILDHOOD, my father never spent any significant amount of time with us. But because of his temper, we did not miss his presence; in fact, his absence often came as a relief. But it happened that, in April of 1969, we were invited to share in a family celebration. Now at the age of 12, I thought that perhaps my father had changed. After all, I had never before seen such generosity in him, and the very thought of having a party brought about great excitement in our home. We waited in eager anticipation for the day to arrive and fantasized over the details.

Finally the day came. The party likely took place only a few days after we received the invitation; however, as a child I remember the time passing incredibly slowly. I woke up early to take extra time in preparing myself; I wanted to ensure that I was thoroughly cleaned and well dressed. When we arrived, we discovered that my father had even slaughtered a goat for the special occasion.

My eyes grew wide as I gazed at all the food spread out before us. My family had grown accustomed to surviving on only a little food; even after eating dinner we were often left feeling unsatisfied, wishing there was more. That was not so with this meal. We were able to eat until we could no longer fit another morsel in our mouths. It was a sensation of feeling full that I had never before experienced. I gorged myself until my dress became tight around the waist.

We all enjoyed ourselves, laughing as we kept going back for more food. And as I looked at the man who had prepared the celebration, I began to wonder if this was truly my father. Could he have changed? I could not comprehend where this newfound generosity had come from, and to my great excitement it did not end with the dinner.

Being raised in a small community with little money, it was not often that we were able to travel, and only rarely did we go into town. But my father had decided to take us to Nakuru, one of the largest towns in the country. City life was much different than what I was used to. I was fascinated with the comings and goings of all the people. I took in as much as I could; there were so many different shops, and I wanted to explore them all.

Though I didn't get to fully indulge in my desire to explore, my father did allow us to go into several shops, where he even bought us new clothing and shoes. I was beside myself with joy. Not only was it the first time my father had ever taken me shopping, but it also was the first time he had purchased something for me.

As we proudly walked down the street with our new parcels in hand, my father had the sudden urge to hire a local photographer to take our family portrait. It was our first family portrait. The photographer explained that we needed to sit as still as we could, and I tried, I really did try. But sitting still is not an easy task for an adventurous girl of my age. Still, I managed to restrain myself long enough to take the portrait, and I made sure I had an extra big grin on my face. I could not believe that we were having our picture taken! My father *had* changed. I thought perhaps something had hit him hard against his head and caused him to become another man. Regardless, I knew something drastic must have happened.

But whatever it was that had caused the change, it did not last. This was the last time my father purchased anything for me, and it was the only picture taken of us as a family. Nothing had hit him hard on the head, although I secretly wished that something had. I now realize that the "family celebration," as my father referred to it, was in fact his way of celebrating the *end* of our family.

My father planned that day, that so-called celebration, in the full knowledge that he would be abandoning my mother. Despite putting my mother through years of suffering, my father had finally become tired of her, and left our family to live with one of his mistresses. The day of joy we had experienced as a family was short lived, and undertaken with terribly impure motives. I cannot imagine what my father was thinking, or his rationale behind the extravagance he showed that day. Perhaps he was trying to buy us off.

Several days after the celebration, my mother was left alone in that little shack in the forest, and I was taken to be a servant for my father's new wife. I did not want to leave my mother—I loved her dearly. My relationship with my father was poor at the best of times, but now I was being forced not only to live with him, but to become a servant to his mistress. I was horrified and wept in despair as my heart ached in pain and sympathy for my mother. How I longed to stay back and comfort her, to hold on to her tightly and tell her that everything would be alright. I desperately desired to stay by her side. But it was as though my father could not hear my cries or see my tears. I was invisible to him; I had already become nothing more than a servant.

My father had given up trying to destroy my mother's faith, but he knew there was still one way he could hurt her most. He knew that if he took us from her she would be devastated. He had no interest in us; he did not love or care for us in the slightest.

To him, we were merely a means to inflict pain and suffering upon our mother. And perhaps he thought he could destroy the religious beliefs our mother had instilled upon us in the process.

However, I was and still remained a stubborn child. I refused to listen to my father and continued to attend church. My actions were not without their consequences; I was continuously beaten, simply because I held strong to the faith my mother had taught me to cherish and regard highly. I didn't care. If my mother could endure this punishment, so too could I.

And I did endure. At the age of 12 my father decided that he wanted me to receive female circumcision, which was and still is the traditional custom of many Kenyan tribes. I had heard horror stories from fellow playmates about the pain associated with this "rite of passage," and the complications that could arise as a result. Imagine the pain one would experience as a razor blade, often as dull as a butter knife, is scraped along the female area until nothing is left. Some girls receive stitches to help the open wound heal; however, these only cause greater complications during intercourse, as the opening is small and tearing occurs.

I decided that I would not allow my father to circumcise me. I did not know how I was going to defy my father's orders, but in my childish stubbornness I had already made up my mind. The rationale behind my defiance was not based on fear of the painful procedure. Rather, I had learned through the Church's teachings that female circumcision was not considered to be a Christian practice. I honestly believed, in my childlike mind, that my mother would burn to death if I was to be circumcised. I do not know where my reasoning originated from—it certainly was not from the Church. But I held strong to my belief. Each time my father brought up the subject I would run around the house screaming, "NO! I will not be circumcised! You just want my mother to burn to death! I WILL NOT ALLOW IT!" I was a determined child with a mind of my own, and eventually my stubbornness prevailed and my father gave up. As a child, I thought I had achieved a great victory; I had saved my mother's life, after all.

✳✳✳✳✳✳✳

Despite my father having forcefully taking me and my siblings away, my mother had not given up. I can only imagine the pain she experienced as her children were taken away from her; the nights she must have spent alone, in tears, her prayers to God filled with sorrow. Yet her faith in God remained unshaken.

> *"We are hard pressed on every side, but not crushed; perplexed, but not in despair; persecuted, but not abandoned; struck down, but not destroyed."* —2 Corinthians 4:8–9

My beloved mother had not given up hope. By the time I was thirteen, she had discovered where my father had taken us, and as soon as she could afford to purchase the bus ticket, she came to beg for our return. My father had always been a man of great rage, but my mother's arrival caused him to go completely wild. She faced great abuse and was severely beaten. But in the face of it all, my mother continued to plead for us to be returned to her. The more she begged, the more he refused, and the more angry and violent his refusals became. Understand that my father did not want us; we were just his way of continuing to inflict pain and sorrow upon my mother. My heart cried out to her. I had missed her so greatly, and all I wanted to do was run toward her, wrap my arms around her and never let her go. But my father refused to let me get near.

In fierce anger, he grabbed hold of my mother's clothing and proceeded toward the fire pit, intending to burn what little she had. My heart could bear it no longer. I quickly grabbed everything I myself possessed, which by this time was not much. I ran toward my parents with my small arms clutching onto a few shabby dresses, and without thinking of the potential danger or the consequences of my actions, I forced myself between the two of them. In a courageous fit of boldness I screamed at my father, "If you burn her clothes you better burn mine as well!"

Though I had great cause to fear, I felt but little. There was always great risk involved when one got between my father's anger and whatever that anger happened to be directed at. There was a strong possibility that his rage would be transferred to the one interrupting, and it was likely that I myself was about to be beaten. Still I would have done anything to protect my mother.

Thankfully, my courage was met with great success, and my father did not burn any clothing, nor did he beat anyone further. We were chased away into the forest, but I thought that was fine; I did not want to be around him anyway.

The forest was cold, and until my mother and I could make our way back to the little shack where I'd grown up, we were forced to go without food or shelter. Despite this, I was thrilled to be reunited with her. I much preferred sleeping in the forest with my mother that night than going back to my father and serving as a slave to his mistress. When daylight came, we returned to the village where my father had left us. We continued to live like this for some time. We would scrounge up whatever edible food source we could find, and did our best to improve our shelter.

It was so hard for my mother. She had to work in other people's gardens in order to raise money to support us. If she was lucky, she was allowed to take raw potatoes and maize back with her, to cook for our dinner. When we had all lived together, and my father was working for the government, we had been living in a very nice, permanent house; we were supplied with everything, even firewood. But after my parents separated, my father moved to another village and we were forced to leave our nice permanent house. We had no choice but to go and live in the shacks the government had built for its subordinate staff.

✳✳✳✳✳✳✳

Finally my father's sister had had enough. She saw what we were going through with my father, and she insisted that a young girl my age required a proper education, and as such, belonged in school. She set out to find me within the forest villages and soon discovered where we were living. She reasoned with my mother about the importance of education and pleaded with me to continue with my schooling. It was hard to leave my mother and my childhood village behind, but one thing I knew was that, if I really wanted to help my mother, I would need to become educated.

I was reluctant to return to my father's house. I feared the beatings and punishments that were sure to come. But there was no way for me to escape; I simply had to return. The house looked much the same, and the very sight of it crushed my heart. At first I refused to enter the house; instead I secretly listened at the door as my aunt spoke to my father with great authority in her voice. She made it clear that he was not to lay a finger on me, and that he was to put an end to this foolish nonsense and send me back to school.

Surprisingly, he listened to her. She was one of the few people who could speak so abruptly to my father without fear. And for one reason or another, he would always listen. He stood there and took her verbal lashing without any retaliation. How I wished she would demand that he send me back to my mother.

I was readmitted to school and went back to serving my father's mistress. Daily life with my father remained next to unbearable. By this time I had only one dress—the others were either outgrown or had become too shabby to continue wearing. I was left with a brown, basic-cut dress.

There was nothing beautiful about this dress. There was nothing about it that flattered my developing body. There were no frills, lace, or ribbons. There wasn't even a shape to the dress; it was a simple, straight-cut brown dress whose sole purpose was to cover my body and nothing more. I might as well have worn a burlap potato sack; there was very little difference between the two. I grew to despise this brown dress, but it was all I had. If I washed it, I had to wear it wet. With each step, the wet brown material would swish and chafe against my body. Oh, how I *hated* that feeling! It was nearly impossible to keep myself clean. Life was truly unbearable.

Of course, the brown dress was only a small contributing factor to my miserable state of mind. It happened that my father's mistress had fallen in love with my younger sister, Mary Mbuiya, and much preferred her over me. Easy to understand; she was an adorable young girl—it was hard not to melt when she gazed at you with her beautiful brown eyes. And in the eyes of my father's mistress, my sister could do no wrong; she could get away with anything.

On its own, this should not have caused me such hardship, but unfortunately my siblings and I did not band together as a family. Rather, our relationship deteriorated as everyone adopted a "survival of the fittest" mentality, and no one did so quicker than my sister. For one reason or another, she loved to pass the blame onto me. In the depths of her imagination, she fabricated countless lies about alleged wrong doings I had committed. She never hesitated to share her creativity with both my father and his mistress, and as they gazed into her sweet, innocent young eyes, they never once doubted the legitimacy of her accusations. I was punished; or rather, doomed. I was distressed by the fact that my sister would stoop to such a low level, but I could not blame her. I understood her motivation; she was simply trying to survive.

I have to give my sister credit, however; she truly did have a good imagination. She could always come up with something. On one occasion, I had received several small booklets from my school teacher. They were a generous gift, one that I was able to take home to keep and cherish. I had never owned anything like these small booklets before, and I was overjoyed and proud of my new possessions. But perhaps I was a little too proud, for these booklets caused my sister to be consumed with jealousy. By the time we returned home, her imagination had already gone to work and created an intricate story regarding how I had supposedly stolen money from a neighbor and used the money to purchase the booklets. She did not hesitate to share her creativity with both my father and his mistress. In my father's rage at this alleged crime, I was beaten throughout the night, his punishment continuing until he himself was too tired to continue. As I huddled to myself in a corner, covered in bruises, I wondered how my sister could have turned against her family so quickly. Was she trying to destroy me, though I had done nothing wrong? I pleaded with my father, and tried to explain that the booklets were a gift from school; however, he would hear none of it.

As I sat there, I realized that my sister was not purposely trying to destroy me. Fabricating lies had simply become her survival tactic: if *I* was being beaten and punished, it meant that she was not. I wondered what trouble she herself had gotten into that day. Why did she need to divert our father's anger toward me? What had *she* done?

❊❊❊❊❊❊❊

Through this episode and numerous similar episodes, my father unknowingly destroyed the childhood relationship I had enjoyed with my siblings. We were together, but we were not a family. And my father's unjustified abuse did not end there; it seemed there was no end to the verbal abuse and embarrassment I endured. It didn't matter where we were or who was around us; he loved to put me down, and seemed to find unnatural joy in publicly humiliating me.

He would often come directly to my school with no other purpose than to verbally abuse me in front of my classmates. Once, he had the teacher pull me aside so that he could scream profanities at me. He even had the audacity to accuse me of prostitution, right there in front of all my fellow schoolmates, making sure that they all heard. I was mortified. I wanted to escape, to hide myself from the verbal lashings shooting out of his mouth. "Make it stop," I thought to myself. But I could neither open my mouth nor defend myself. I was forced to just stand there and take the abuse. I would rather he had beat me, but he had to restrain himself while we were still in the school.

I do not understand why he was so upset, or why he felt the need to come to the school—he must have had a bad morning. His screams of rage were loud enough for the entire school to hear. When he had finally finished and stormed off the school property, I was left to face my class. In pure embarrassment, I slunk back to my desk and kept my head down. "How dare he?" I thought; I had done nothing wrong.

But then I was reminded of my dear mother, who had endured such hardships all for her faith in the Lord. I stopped sulking in my desk and sat upright.

I knew I had to be strong.

SELF-SACRIFICE

I T WAS AT the age of 15 that I realized my formal education had reached its end. I no longer needed to beg for money to meet school fees, nor did I need to continue serving my father's mistress. And with this realization came a deeper understanding of my future—I was going to be okay. I realized that one day I would be married and that my future would be stable.

Late one evening, while I was deep in sleep, I had a dream about the future I was to have. I felt there was to be great peace in my future, despite not being able to complete my education. I came to realize that God had something else in store for me. I knew I had a higher calling. And within that same dream, my brother's future was revealed as well, though his future would follow a different path. He was never going to marry; instead, his education was of key importance. I felt that if my brother became educated, then he would be able to look after my mother, helping her to lead a happier life. And so I forfeited my education for his, and did so with a sense of relief; now I knew that everything would be okay.

But with that relief came a sense of duty. I believed that the burden of ensuring that my brother received a proper education fell upon my shoulders. I submitted this responsibility to much thought and prayer. Continuously, I asked myself what I could possibly do to force my father to pay for my brother's schooling. Finally, I realized the drastic measure I had to take.

I had to run away from my father's abuse and oppression. I knew that this action would cause our father to be overcome with guilt, guilt which would in turn ensure the proper education of my brother. I realize now that the solution I decided on was childish and poorly thought out, but at the time I believed it to be the master plan to achieving my goal. With this key piece of knowledge and my sense of profound understanding, I began to plan my escape—the same escape that would save my brother's future.

It was in January 1973 at the age of 16, during the heat of the Kenyan summer, that I had finally had enough. My father had beaten me through the night in another one of his unjustified moments of rage. The following morning I was given only a small portion of sugarless, watered-down porridge for breakfast. I was not allowed to sit at the table and join the rest of the household; instead, I was to drink the watered-down slop from the corner, as I watched everyone else indulge in what appeared to be a breakfast feast. The smell alone was enough to drive a hungry girl mad. I could no longer bear it—now was the time.

This was the end of my relationship with my father. It was also at this time that I reunited with my mother. This was something I had long wished for: I had missed her greatly, and had decided that I would rather live a poor life at her side than continue to be a servant to my father's mistress, whom I saw as nothing less than the woman who had destroyed my family. It only seemed natural for me to escape my father's household and run directly to my mother; where else would I have gone?

But while she was thrilled to see me, I had returned to her during a desperate time. Our life together during this time was not without hardship, and money was not readily available. However, for the first time in many years, I was happy.

As for my brother, the school fees my father had been putting toward my education were now used for my brother's. My brother continued to receive the brunt of the abuse from my father, but his perseverance would eventually pay off. I He finished Grade 12 with high marks, and was admitted to the Kabaa Boys High School for two years. After passing high school with distinction, he was able to secure a place at Nairobi University, where he studied geology. Today, he is an Engineer for the Ministry of Natural Resources. True to my prayers, he built a fine home for my mother and takes good care of her.

******

Unfortunately, my time with my mother was short lived. She could not afford to keep me, and I was sent to live with one of my aunts.

But for one reason or another, no one was interested in keeping me, and I was gradually passed along from one relative to another.

I remember one aunt in particular—my time with her was especially difficult. Aunt Rebeca Wangari was a firm believer in hard work, and I was set to work for her from dawn to dusk. I worked long hours each day, until every bone in my body ached. My fingers and feet became tired and callused. But I was not alone; her own children were expected to work just as hard. For them, work was their life; it was all they knew. The children had been so neglected that they had become plagued with jiggers on their feet and throughout their body. Jiggers are insects that crawl into the skin and eat away at the body's flesh, leaving open sores which are prone to infection. The children had suffered from these jiggers for years, and their bodies had become unpleasantly deformed as a result. They were covered in open wounds and walked with a crooked limp. With proper medical attention the jiggers could have been removed and future infections prevented, but sadly my aunt was so focused on work and her daily tasks that she refused to "waste" valuable time stopping to help her children heal.

I was horrified and feared that I would catch jiggers myself, but at that time there was nowhere else for me to go. And so I stayed, and worked hard to earn my keep; not a moment of daylight was allowed to be wasted. As each day passed, my heart went out to my cousins, who struggled and were left to slave away, day in and day out. They were only children, kept from school and forced into hard labor at too young an age. I knew that without any education, their future was bleak at best; and for the moment, so was mine.

As I observed my cousins hobbling along during their daily tasks, I wondered how any mother could care so little for her children. But eventually their mother realized that she too could not afford to keep me. A young burden upon my family, it was not long before I had been passed off to another relative. While transfers such as this became a common occurrence, it was rare for me to experience this much relief at going to live with another family member. I thanked God that I did not have to stay a moment longer. And I thanked God that I did not contract jiggers.

Things continued like this for a while, until eventually there was nowhere left for me to turn. I had gradually worked my way through my relatives, until they had all decided that they could not keep me. It was not as though I was causing trouble or not doing my share of the chores, it was simply that no one had enough money to afford to feed an extra child.

But rejection can be hard to bear, especially for a young girl. This was by no means an easy time for me. Many of my relatives chose to look down on me. No one believed that there was potential in this young schoolgirl runaway, and I was continually harassed by belittling verbal comments. But in my prideful stubbornness, I continued to stand up for myself. I would tell them of my faith in God, and how through Him I would one day make something of myself. I knew that one day I would become extraordinary. I trusted that God had something set aside for me, and I knew that one day they would come to respect me. Still, as young as I was, there was nowhere left for me to go, no one else to turn to, and the thought of returning back to my father's household was out of the question. I accepted my life's circumstances and began to seek independence through employment as a household servant.

No one within my family had any objections to my seeking employment; in fact, it was a relief for them to know that they no longer had to support me. It was not long before I was able to find a suitable employer. For the first time in my life, I had achieved true independence, and I began to enjoy being self-reliant. My employer was a well-respected man who had worked his way up within a large Kenyan broadcasting organization. He and his family treated me exceptionally well; I was well fed, and even provided with clothing. Unlike my family, they did not harass or taunt me. I began to realize just how poorly my family had treated me, and I questioned why they had taken such advantage of my situation. Aside from my mother, I did not mind being away from family. Besides, I didn't want jiggers.

The family was wonderful. My main responsibility was to watch after the children, but I was also helping with household chores when necessary. However, it happened that my employer was a member of the Muslim faith. This did not seem to cause conflict between him and myself, despite my being Christian. But unfortunately, I was only employed for two months before my extended family came to realize that my employer was Muslim, and feared that I myself would convert to his faith. For this reason, they joined together to bring me back, despite previously wanting nothing to do with me. They had shown such little concern over my troubles and hardships, forcing me into finding employment as a maid at such a young age. And now they demanded that I return home with them. I could not see the justification in their actions, nor did I understand why they took such a great concern over the matter. However, in respect to my elders, I left my employment with the family and returned to live in my family's village.

What was I to do? No one wanted me to join their household, yet the moment I gained independence and was able to support myself, they cried out in rage and demanded that I return. But return to what, to whom? They had each pushed me away, claiming that I was too great a financial burden. My despair and frustration over my life's circumstances was beginning to swell. My place in the world was not yet established; in fact I felt as though I did not have a place. As I listened to every argument over where I was to stay, my self-confidence weakened, until I felt completely alone in the world. The self-pride to which I had once held strong was being demolished. Maybe I was *not* destined for greatness after all; perhaps I was simply an uneducated hindrance to my family.

Finally, after intense family debate, it was decided that the burden of my presence was to fall upon my grandmother. The entire situation was too much to bear; while I did love my grandmother and I enjoyed her presence greatly, the fierce disputes I had caused in my family led to my being overwhelmed with anguished embarrassment.

Eventually I settled into my grandmother's home and began to work hard to help with the household chores. By this time I had become accomplished in embroidery and put my talent to good use for the benefit of my grandmother. I was still a young teenager of eligible school-age, but by this point completing my education was not an option. My grandmother provided me with basic food and shelter, but that was not enough to meet my needs. From my brief time as a household servant, I had grown accustomed to receiving a paycheck, in addition to room and board. I was working just as hard, but now I had to go without pay. I began to feel cheated, as though my hard work was being taken advantage of. Feeling alone and in despair, I became embittered toward the world.

My dream of becoming a prominent name in Kenya had been crushed. The entire ordeal was a huge blow to my self-esteem, and worse, I had begun to see myself though my family's eyes—as nothing more than an unwanted burden.

My life had begun a downward spiral.

AGAINST ALL ODDS

I T HAD BEGUN with my having become an undesired burden
upon my family. My mother, amazing woman that she was,
still could not help but see a burden when she looked at me;
a cherished and beloved burden, but a burden all the same. I
worked hard and never once caused trouble, yet I was still passed
from one relative to the next, until there was no one left. Of
course I took it personally. Even when I became self-reliant and
began to support myself, my family was unhappy. There was no
pleasing them.

My family's intense arguments over who was to take responsibility for me were difficult to bear. Even my time with my
grandmother did not come without its own troubles. At first,
everything seemed to go well; but gradually I began to long for
the independence I had tasted all too briefly during my employment. As I grew, my needs went beyond basic food and shelter,
and I began to long for more from my life. I wanted—or in my
opinion, needed—to receive a paycheck for my labors. But more
than that, I needed to establish my independence.

At this realization, I broke down into tears and sobbed for
hours. I was frustrated with life. I did not know what to do or
where to go, although I knew that it was time for me to regain
my independence. But with my self-worth crushed under the
weight of my family's scorn, I gave up hope; in despair, I ran off

to accept employment wherever I could find it. In the end, I became the manager of a small, shabby bar.

It was around this time that I discovered my beauty. For one reason or another, the opposite sex was drawn toward me. Up to this point, I had not been oblivious to the prolonged glances cast in my direction; but it was around this time that those awkward, unwanted glances developed into something more. It became common for men to offer cattle or goats in exchange for my hand in marriage. Imagine the nerve of a complete stranger, offering such a proposition! They assumed I could be purchased, like a possession. True, this is not uncommon within the Kenyan culture; however, I wanted nothing to do with it. I had no use for a husband. I cherished my newfound independence. Besides, upon questioning, I discovered that most of the men were from the rift valley, and there are far too many donkeys in the rift valley.

Looking back, I realize that I may have been too unmannerly and rude to my potential suitors. However, I felt the need to state my independence clearly, and make it known to all that I could not be bought. I was not interested. I even had a daring mother approach me on behalf of her unnamed son to propose marriage. Had I ever met her son? Who knew. Like all the proposals I received at that time, it was quickly turned down and brushed aside, with a hint of a sly grin upon my face. I never took any of the proposals seriously; rather, the courting process became a fabulous game of entertainment for me.

This immature amusement only continued upon accepting employment in a bar. The marriage offers increased, save that now many of these offers were proposed in an ungraceful, drunken slur. Even more entertaining, I thought.

I was not employed at the bar for long, however, when a man approached me and explained that a woman such as myself should

AGAINST ALL ODDS

not be working in a bar. He claimed to see the dangers I didn't, and argued that it was not a suitable place for me to be in. The man appeared distinguished and was more gentlemanly than the average customer I was used to dealing with. He described with pride the mining plant he owned and operated in Voi. The way in which he spoke led me to believe that the plant would be an excellent place of employment, and surprisingly, there happened to be an open secretarial position! He inquired as to whether or not I would be interested. I was not sure, but he persisted, going on at length about the plant's benefits.

I must admit, I *had* already grown tired of working in a bar. The drunken proposals were fun at first, but I soon became bored with the game. I was relieved to hear of a new job opportunity, especially one with better pay which would allow me to maintain my dignity. At the time, I felt as though I had given the matter significant consideration, and believed I had weighed each benefit and drawback within my mind. But truthfully, I had made my decision in a matter of seconds. It did not take him long to convince me to leave.

But the secretarial position really did seem ideal. The man, a mere stranger, even offered to transport me to the mine location. I gathered my few belongings together and bounced to the car, dreaming of my new start in life.

In my youthful innocence, I was all too easily persuaded by this gentleman. As we sat in his car, all I could think about was my new position as a secretary, and it was with great anticipation that I waited to arrive at my final destination. Never once did I question the existence of the mining plant that was so eloquently described to me.

Thankfully, the plant *was* there. True, it was neither as grand nor as spectacular as he made it out to be, but it did not fall too far from his description. He provided me with an adequate place to stay, and I unpacked my belongings, already dreaming of my secretarial job. What exactly had I been hired to do? I did not have an answer to that question, but I used my imagination to fill in the blanks. I thought my life had really made a change for the better—I was becoming *someone*. I was no longer a family burden, and I could already feel my sense of self-worth growing.

But the feeling quickly wore off as I discovered what my secretarial responsibilities truly entailed. His ulterior motive hit me like a slap across the face. He had no need for a secretary; he wanted me as his second wife, and did not hesitate to take advantage of me.

He was no different than the drunken fools who had slurred their proposals vaguely in my direction. Well, there was one difference: he had managed to successfully fool me.

No longer did I view him as a gentleman; rather, he had become a dirty snake whose very touch repulsed me. How could I have been so foolish? I had no desire to marry this man. He already had a wife and children of his own; he merely wanted to gain the cultural prestige of having taken a second wife. I could not, *would not,* be a trophy; nor could I be responsible for damaging an existing marriage.

Unfortunately, I was trapped. The mining plant was far from any town and, as I was without money, I had no choice but to stay employed as his "secretary." There was no way for me to leave, even as he continued to force himself on me. It was not long before everyone at the mining plant heard of my situation. I suspect some, in a joking sort of tone, congratulated their boss for capturing a new mistress, but most took no concern over the matter. Yet there was one soft heart, one compassionate elderly woman who came to hear of my story and took great pity on me.

She herself had very little, but led by her sympathy she purchased a bus ticket for me to return home. She became my saving grace.

Once safely on the bus bound for home, I wondered privately how many other young girls had fallen into a similar situation. How many had he fooled and held captive?

Back in my home village, I discovered that nothing had changed. It was disorienting; though I had not been gone long, within that time my life had been completely altered. I half expected that everything else would have changed as well. Yet it had not. Not yet ready to return to my relatives and not yet willing to ask them for help, I sought out a friend I had come to know during my stay in Voi—the business partner of the very same gentleman who had lured me there in the first place. I had often shared my personal problems with her; she told me that, were I ever to succeed in running away from the plant, she would give me a place to stay in her home in Ngong.

Following the directions she had given me, I went to her house and was welcomed in and introduced to her family. I lived with her for a short time after that, but it soon became apparent that she would not be able to support me on her own. I pleaded with her to employ me as a member of the household help—that way, the money she normally spent on servants could be put toward my room and board. We were able to continue with this arrangement for the rest of the year, but by the end, we were both tired, and I was still feeling discouraged.

Rather than turn me out into the street, she instead rented a small room for me in the Kerarapon shopping center in Ngong, and handed me the keys, saying that she had paid for two month's rent up-front; the rest was up to me. But at this time, I was a broken woman. The bright future I had imagined for myself, that had sustained me throughout my childhood, was beginning to dim and disappear before my eyes. I had nowhere to turn, no prospect of employment, and no family to count on. In great discouragement, I had given up on life.

I decided to become a prostitute.

But still, I did not have the heart of a prostitute. I could not do the things they did. My heart did not allow me to fully submit to the sexual immorality and lust with which I had surrounded myself. I remember looking at the lives of the prostitutes I associated with, wondering how they did it. And thankfully, God protected me and forbid me from becoming pregnant.

It felt as though I had abandoned my body. I had mentally removed myself from the immorality surrounding me. In despair I degraded myself, and in doing so I had become part of it. Or had I? Was that truly me, there in the midst of it all? I had reached a point of desperation, with no hope of turning back. There was nowhere to turn back to. I began to submit myself to the lewdness of offering my very being for a profit. I simply gave up on life.

But God had not given up.

You yourself may be wondering why anyone actively involved in ministry, as I am now, would be so willing to admit to the past sins of their life. But while it was a time in my life that I am not proud of, it only proves that I am human, and have great faults of my own. And that it is only through God's saving grace that I have been able to overcome the sins of my past and move forward on my spiritual walk. I praise God for the darkest hours of my life, for they enabled me to understand those who have come from a life of sin. I know how easy it is to fall, and how wonderful it is to regain one's relationship with God.

Looking back, I wonder: how could anyone put a price on something so precious? Would we really, in hungered desperation, do anything for money? For one hot meal? Understand that I did not reach this point of future regret overnight; rather, it was the culmination of a series of events that had led me to spiral down to such a level of grotesque immorality. I was brought to a point of utter despair and hopelessness.

At the time I refused to attend Church—I pushed God far from my life and chose instead to walk the path most opposed to His. I thought I had truly pushed him away, but while I no longer felt His presence at the time, I now understand that He was still close.

It was during this dark moment of my life that I walked by an open-air service. Some man, claiming to be ordained by God, had chosen a random street corner to preach from. The street was not exceptionally clean, nor was it the busiest street in the community—there were far better location choices he could have made. But he chose to preach on the very street I was walking on. I went to pass by the crowd gathered around the preacher, but my feet would not allow it. I wanted to continue on my way; still I was drawn in. Before I knew what was going on, several individuals began to pray over me, laying their hands on me and asking God to heal me. Little did I know that those prayers would change my destiny.

Understand that I still believed in God; I just wanted nothing to do with Him. My life no longer resembled that of a Christian; rather it had become the life of one without faith or hope. I had already tried to give my life over to alcohol and prostitution, but God was holding me up to something higher. The prayer that came over me at that moment was overwhelmingly intense. The very next day I was offered two jobs; most importantly, I was offered an escape from the life I had been trying to throw myself into.

My history is simply that—history. I now had two jobs before me, both offering life-changing, life-saving opportunities. One position was too far for me to travel to daily, so my choice was simple, and I openly accepted the second job offer. I gained employment with a gas station, where I was responsible for selling gas and convenience items. I was able to live with an older woman, who lived within walking distance from the gas station. Though I could not have known it at the time, this woman was to become my future sister-in-law.

Nor did I realize at the time that each day, as I walked to work, I was passing by my future husband, Isaac. In fact, I did not take any notice of him until he became a regular at the gas station. Each day he would come in to purchase a soda, and occasionally the newspaper. I became a little suspicious of his presence—either the man had a seriously unhealthy soda addiction, or he was coming for more than just soda. Meetings with Isaac became a daily ritual as he continued his supposed over-consumption of soda. He even had the nerve to follow me home one day.

I was irritated, to say the least. Here was a man, significantly older than myself, relentlessly pursuing me. By now I knew that it was not just the soda that he wanted. But no matter how hard I tried, I could not deter his persistence. The man was truly relentless.

After two months of working at my new job, I started having problems with my housemate, Isaac's sister. She felt that I was not helping out enough around the house we shared with her family, and tensions began to rise between us. Things came to a head one evening, when she demanded to know why I had left the house a mess. I told her that I had been waiting until the family was asleep before I started to clean, but she took this to be just another excuse, and threw me out of the house. It was raining that night, and without anywhere else to go, I sought out the only person I felt I could trust—Isaac.

Like the prodigal son, I went looking for him, only to finally locate him in a Ngong night club. When I saw him, he was surprised, and asked me what I was doing in the night club. I couldn't help it; I just started crying, telling him my problems. I told him that I was not ready to be cheated by another man, and that if he was not going to marry me then and there, he should leave me alone. I was leaving him with no choice, but because he loved me, he took the risk of marrying me and from there we started our new life together.

A two-month courtship may seem short, but it is important to understand this within the context of Kenyan culture. His last test was fulfilling the requirements I had set down as a nine-year-old child. Thankfully, he passed; Isaac was not from the rift-valley.

And he did not own a donkey!

RECONNECTING WITH GOD

G OD HAD ANSWERED my prayers. He had given me not only a husband, but a friend and a companion, someone who would both listen to my problems and walk my path alongside me. He loved me, and he did not look down on me for my weaknesses.

However, it turned out that soda wasn't the only thing that Isaac liked to drink, and before long I had an unhealthy drinking habit to match his own. We continued on like this, until one day the two of us became drunk and started fighting. It was the first time we had fought, and for me, it served as a harsh wake-up call. The following morning, once I'd sobered up, I realized that I would not be able to build a home for myself if I continued drinking. I told Isaac that I had decided to give up alcohol completely, and that I was leaving him. I would return home, to the house my mother took me to.

But it wasn't long before I relented and returned to Isaac, having decided instead to help him defeat his drinking habits, and get them under control. We each brought our struggles into this marriage, but that just meant we would need to overcome them together. We took off on a bumpy road and were uncertain of our destination, but after all, I still loved him very much, and knew that, within time, the two of us could create a beautiful home together.

Within time, and by working together, both Isaac and I cleaned up our lives. Isaac was able to at last overcome his battle with alcohol, and although he chose not to attend services at the church, he still came when our children Caroline and Sialo were being baptized. I abandoned my past and became actively involved in the PCEA Church in Ngong, and shortly after became a Sunday school teacher, youth leader, and member of the Women's Guild. In 1981, through the help of a mutual friend who was a former member of Parliament, Isaac was also reinstated to his former position as a Veterinary Technician in the Ministry of Livestock and Agriculture.

It was also around this time that I rediscovered the importance of faith. My personal relationship with the Lord had been restored, and I was once again inspired by the example my mother had set for me, so many years before.

My life is anything but perfect; I am merely human. But by God's grace, He still chose to use me to further His work.

WHO CAN BE AGAINST US?

"Those He predestined, he also called; those He called, he also justified; those He justified, He also glorified. What then shall we say in response to this? If God is for us, who can be against us?"

—Romans 8:30

THE VISION OF creating a children's home did not come to me instantaneously.

Even after my marriage to Isaac, I was uncertain as to where God would direct my life. Isaac and I continued to strengthen the bond between us, as we grew together in the Lord. Soon after our difficulties were resolved, we were blessed with our first child, Caroline born on April 12, 1980. But little more than a year later, shortly after I became pregnant with my second daughter, Catherine, I began to suffer serious health issues, which eventually turned out to be degenerative heart disease. Doctors recommended I stay on complete bed rest in the hospital, and placed me on heart therapy medicine.

For six months, I remained in the hospital, but when the time came to deliver my daughter, the doctors found that my smaller-than-average cervix combined with my fragile heart made a natural birth unsafe. They recommended that I deliver through operation, and on October 4, 1982, I delivered a beautiful baby girl weighing 3.5 kilograms. I was released from hospital after two weeks of post-op care, and began attending a heart health clinic.

The doctors tried to advise me against having any more children, citing my heart condition as cause for concern. But I refused; like any African woman, I wanted a family of six children. I was soon pregnant again. It was around this time that it really struck home for me just how sick I was. I was again admitted to the hospital and marked for another for six months stay until delivery. It was difficult, leaving my children and my husband alone. I couldn't risk doing that to them again, let alone risk greater injury to myself. While I was in the hospital, preparing to deliver my third child, I made the difficult decision to receive tubal ligation and remove the possibility of becoming pregnant. My ideal of having six children would never be.

It was a difficult delivery. Twice I was taken to the operating room for an elective cesarean section, it still not being safe to deliver naturally. But each time, we found no doctors there to perform the operation. During this time, the doctors in the area were on strike, demanding better conditions and more resources. The few doctors who *were* there refused to touch me, saying that if anything were to go wrong, there would be no one to protect them from cries of negligence. Things quickly came to a head on the morning of September 10, 1984, when my labor pains were so great that doctors were brought in from the intensive care unit to perform my operation. I was medicated for my pain, though I remained conscious of what was going on around me. The operation was performed successfully, but when it came time to revive me, the doctors discovered that the necessary medication was nowhere to be found. I heard one of them say, "The work we have done is for nothing. She is going, she is going, she is gone..."

I did not have a problem with dying; I knew that what awaited me was a world far brighter than my own, and so I had no fear of death. But as I lay there on the operating table, drifting away, I thought of my two children, Caroline and Catherine. I had seen what life was like for children without their parents around; like a flash, I became determined that I would not die, that this was not my time. At that moment, I recalled a verse in Proverbs 18, which said "Death and life are in the power of the tongue." If I want to die, I can die; but if I wish to live, I will live. I chose then to live for the sake of children, my own included.

At that moment, I heard the doctors saying, "The pulse is there, the pulse is there! Run for it, run for it!" I opened my eyes, and realized that God had given me a new lease on life. Like the woman who touched the hem of Jesus, I had been healed.

When I was released from the hospital, I started doing all the things I could not do previously, and I found that my heart was not affected. I realized that healing is divine; it can only be given by God. In a moment of excitement, I told God I would like to thank him by adopting a child without parents or food into our home. Little did I realize, I was laying the foundation for what would become the Huruma Children's Home and School in Ngong.

A friend of mine, who worked with a local organization called the National Christian Churches of Kenya, helped me to develop a proposal aimed at gaining support for my vision, and in 1985, the project was sponsored by a large international organization working to provide funding to nourish local children. It was only a small step toward my ultimate goal, but I was thrilled to be working toward the calling God had put in my heart. To maintain accountability, I thought it wise to involve as many local churches as possible; the resulting program was thus titled The

Ngong Churches Huruma Project. And it was me, an uneducated woman, who was to be responsible for developing the project and properly managing the funding received.

Sadly, it was the case that many of the children within our neighborhood came from poor families where they were abused, neglected and malnourished. In addition to the feeding program, we began a vocational training program for local women. Here, women were taught the important skills needed to gain employment. They were also encouraged to turn away from substance abuse and focus on improving their lives and caring for their families. I was also able to institute a weekly Bible study within the local community, which gave me the opportunity to minister to the children, and teach them about their faith.

I was extremely busy, but I knew the Lord was using me to do His work. Still, I began to feel uneasy regarding the stability of my position. I began to wonder whether I truly had the support of my church and community. I approached the pastor of my church to ask him for help and guidance; unfortunately, my troubles were not well received. I came to him with my Bible in hand, hoping to receive spiritual guidance, yet I was told to put away the Word of God and "think for myself."

And this was the advice of a pastor!

I asked him: "What do *you* preach from? What pastor does not use the Bible?!" I was furious, and refused to listen to the guidance of my supposed church leader. For just the night before, God had spoken to me through scripture. The Lord had guided me to the biblical story of Ahaz, King of Judah, found within the book of Isaiah. Ahaz was under attack; two powerful forces had aligned themselves in the hopes of overtaking him. It was at this time that the Lord spoke to Isaiah, and told Isaiah to encourage Ahaz.

Unlike Ahaz, I did not know of the battle that lay before me. But God had full knowledge of the troubles I would soon be experiencing, and I believe the Lord chose to use the words of Isaiah to personally encourage me:

"Be careful, keep calm and don't be afraid." —Isaiah 7:4

I did not yet know of the secret meetings being held, nor the plot developing against me, but I soon learned that the community no longer supported my involvement in the Ngong Churches Huruma Project. Even my church's pastor had become involved in the schemes; this is why he had no concern for my troubles, and offered me such poor advice.

My work was in a slum of Kenya. It was a very poor neighborhood, and many of those who lived there were slaves to one form of substance abuse or another. Several of these individuals were financially bribed to taunt me, in an effort to destroy the project left in my care. I even received a warning from a friend not to eat any food given to me by the community for fear that they would try to poison me. But still I refused to give in or back down. I held strong, and God continued to speak to me through the words of Isaiah.

"Do not lose heart because of these two smoldering stubs of
firewood—because of the fierce anger of Rezin and Aram
and of the son of Remaliah. Aram, Ephraim and Remaliah's
son have plotted your ruin, saying, 'Let us invade Judah; let
us tear it apart and divide it among ourselves, and make the
son of Tabeal king over it.'" —Isaiah 7:4–6

I was determined not to lose heart. The community had become the two smoldering stubs of firewood that stood in my path. They plotted my ruin, as I came to discover, because I refused to misuse the money designated to the Ngong Churches Huruma Project. Many felt they were entitled to a portion of the funding the project received from the large international organization. And so they searched for opportunities to tear the Project apart and divide the funding among themselves.

Since I refused to mismanage the finances, they wanted to put someone else in charge—someone who would redirect money from the Project into the pockets of corrupt community members. Soon, even some member churches became involved in the scheme, which put considerable pressure on me. They too believed they were entitled to a portion of the funding. I faced daily harassment and abuse from both the community and the church, as each did their best to tarnish my name. But I held strong and continued on in the work God had entrusted to my care. When I was faced with their abuse, I turned to God for my strength; again and again, He comforted me and told me that they could not bring me down.

> *"Yet this is what the Sovereign Lord says: 'It will not take place, it will not happen.'"*—Isaiah 7:7

Finally, I was directly accused of being a thief. Vicious rumors spread throughout the community that I was withholding financial support from the organization and pocketing the funds for my own personal gain. Things didn't really come to a head, however, until I was approached by a group of seven children who wanted to go to school. They explained that they, like many of the children on the streets, have no home or shelter of any kind;

they truly have nowhere to go. And without some kind of roof over their heads, they wouldn't be able to go to school.

I approached the office of the Ministry of Social Services in Ngong, asking for help in seeing that these children received the education they needed. Unfortunately, this simple act prompted a series of events that would lead to my termination as administrator of the Project. The board governing the Project was advised to terminate my employment, explaining that, being illiterate, I was ill-suited to run the Project that I had helped to start. After letting me go, the program was transferred to the PCEA Church in Ngong, the same congregation that I myself belonged to.

Because I had refused to share the funds meant for the children with the church leaders and community members, they fabricated these false accusations and had me removed as director of the project, making clear their way to gain access to the funds for their own purposes. But unfortunately, their actions caused the entire project to be revoked; soon after my termination, the project was brought to an end. Funding for the Ngong Churches Huruma Project was no longer available.

And what's worse, without those finances, local children were not being provided with daily nutrition and the woman's vocational training was cancelled. I was labeled as a con, a thief, a devil worshiper, and a mad woman, all because I held true to my word and did not redirect any of the funding received. The community went so far as to hold a mock burial for me. Picture a church community, burying a physical coffin for a living breathing person. And they called *me* a mad woman! To this day, I have no idea what they buried inside the coffin bearing my name. But praise God, I found my strength in Him who forbid them from bringing me to my ruin. In the words of Isaiah:

"If you do not stand firm in your faith, you will not stand at all." —Isaiah 7:9

Who can be against you? Many can be against you. But what I came to learn is that God will always give you the strength to persevere. No earthly power outweighs the power of God. Throughout my life I was put down, but His call was greater. As I worked for the Lord, there would be times when many were against me. I was following the passion that the Lord had put on my heart—a great love for children; but still the community had turned against me. I was persecuted and falsely accused of wrongdoings.

They had successfully brought an end to my role in the Ngong Churches Huruma Project, and even the project itself. But they did not bring an end to the vision God had put in my heart. Even so, I still had to address the original cause of this whole mess—seven young children, still living on the street, who were in need of a place to call home while they pursued an education. The desire to help underprivileged children continued to burn within me, and it was with a steady sense of purpose that I petitioned the courts to grant me custody of the children and responsibility for their well-being. They found me to be a fit guardian, and I found myself with ten children to call my own, rather than three.

But now that funding was no longer available, and there was no government housing that I could use to start the school, I was forced to search for alternative means. I decided that, with the little money I had left, I would buy several lottery tickets. I was desperate; the children needed proper nutrition and I no longer had the financial support necessary to provide it for them. Upon purchasing the tickets, I spent several days in fasting and prayer.

I was certain that God would provide for the children. After all, how could a loving God allow children to experience hunger pains and malnutrition on a daily basis? He certainly would not let them go without.

I truly believed that those lottery tickets would be God's method of provision. I fasted in heartbroken tears for several days, until finally in prayer I opened the lottery tickets. I found nothing; I had not won a single shilling.

As I sat on my bed, I began to cry, wondering what I would do, and how I would feed all the children. It was then that I heard a voice, cautioning me not to give into panic or despair. This voice jolted me back to life. I had forgotten to truly put my trust in God's plan. I must trust in Him. My faith must be in Him alone. God used this experience to teach me a lesson: While I did not know how things would work out; I put God in control. And, in faith, I knew He would provide for our needs.

I found further comfort through Scripture when God spoke to me through Job 14:7–9:

> *"At least there is hope for a tree: If it is cut down, it will sprout again, and its new shoots will not fail. Its roots may grow old in the ground and its stump die in the soil, yet at the scent of water it will bud and put forth shoots like a plant."*

I had been cut down, but I was to wait with patience for the water of God. I was to wait for my own growth; the realization of my vision was still to come. I was encouraged to remain strong in my faith, and continue to hold strong; for God had not abandoned me or my ever-growing family.

For there is a hope of a tree
If it be cut down
That it will sprout again
The tender branches will not cease

Though the root grow old in the ground
And the stock die in the soil
Yet through the feat of water
The tree will bud up again.

Trust in the Lord and do good,
So that thou may dwell in the land
And verily you shall be fed
And be given the desires of your heart.
—Job 14:7–9

FOLLOWING WHERE HE LEADS

D ESPITE THE HARDSHIPS I faced, I continued to remain
strong in my life of prayer. During this time, I was also an
unwavering member of an international women's prayer group
called Aglow International. Despite the rumors put out by the
community, the prayer group's chapter in Kenya elected me to
attend an international conference as a representative of Kenya,
the theme of which was, "Ordinary Women with Extraordinary
Callings." While I had never before experienced international
travel, as I was still in the midst of hardship and persecution at
home, I decided not to pass up the opportunity God had put
before me. Leaving would present me with the opportunity to
think, and regain perspective. And so, with the help of sponsorship, I ventured off to San Antonio, Texas.

Unfortunately, as it was my first experience with leaving the
country, I was overwhelmed and confused. Having received my
passport, I was trying to make my way to the airline ticket coun-
ter, but many individuals surrounded me, with ill intentions. An
international flight ticket and passport are hard to attain in Kenya.
Because of this, many individuals wanted to defraud me of both
the ticket and passport, and travel to America themselves. There
was too much confusion; I felt as though I was surrounded on all
sides by a whirlwind.

I knew nothing of international travel and must have appeared
very foolish. Finally, the flight attendant was so confused that she

demanded everyone leave, save for the original ticket holder: me. The entire process took considerably longer than it should have, and the airline spent so much time clearing up the confusion that they were forced to delay the flight for me personally. Finally, with ticket firmly in hand, an attendant was assigned to direct me toward the appropriate terminal. By this time it was obvious to all that I had never flown before, and the last thing they wanted was for me to get lost, further postponing the flight. So, like a child, I was escorted through the halls.

This is also when I—for the first time in my life—encountered moving stairs. I was terrified! My heart rate increased and I was filled with the fear of the unknown. I had no idea how to enter an escalator, nor did I have any desire to learn. But unfortunately, in order to catch the plane and travel to America, I had no choice. I stood there, watching each step come and go. Each time, just as I began to work up the courage to jump on a stair, it would move forward and away, and another would appear before me. Finally, I counted to three, closed my eyes and forced myself to board the escalator. By this time the flight attendant had become rather annoyed and felt the need to lend a "helpful" push.

Even aboard the escalator my heart continued to pound. I was fascinated by the invention, but I was just as unsure of how to get *off* the moving stairs as I had been with getting on. Fortunately, I was relieved to discover how easy it was, and once I had safely disembarked I couldn't help but stand there, laughing—not only because of the unnecessary fear I had experienced over moving stairs, but because I also now had to wait for my shoes to arrive, several steps behind me. To this day, I still do not understand how they were left behind; but I will never forget my first encounter with an escalator.

I learned a lot on my first international trip, and had the opportunity to experience many new things. But while much happened during my time in the United States, what I remember best is the guidance that God provided me with. While at the conference, I had the opportunity to speak with the keynote speaker. She spoke of the many strong women of the Bible and their callings—Sarah, Rebecca, Ruth, Naomi, Debra and Mary, mother of Jesus. They all looked so ordinary, and yet were each extraordinary in their ability to realize God's plan for them. I began to realize that, despite my own ordinary appearance, I too had received an extraordinary calling. Despite being without status or education, I still was called to do extraordinary things. She quoted the Scriptures then, and I truly believe that it was the Lord speaking to me through him:

> *"Be still before the Lord and wait patiently for him; do not fret when men succeed in their ways, when they carry out their wicked schemes."* —Psalm 37:7

I was to be still and trust in my Lord. It was He who had called me and given me such a large vision—if I was to wait patiently, He would see me through my difficulties. This was much easier said than done; it is hard not to worry when a wicked scheme against you appears to have been successful. But I knew now: I was to remain still and persevere in faith, trusting that God would provide and knowing that He would not allow the community to tarnish my name.

But he never told me how long I would wait. That was the hardest time in my life when I was reduced to a puddle of tears. And still children were now coming, and I could not chase the children away.

Mama Zipporah
with her brother,
mother, and a friend
in front of their
former home.

Mama Zipporah and her husband on their wedding day, with their daughters,
Catherine Sialo Butt and Caroline Naiserian.

Mama Zipporah with her first group of children at Huruma Children's Home.

*Mama Zipporah with two former children
of Huruma Children's Home.*

*The first school at Huruma
Children's Home.*

Mama Zipporah giving former Vice President Moody Awori a tour of Huruma Children's Home.

Mama Zipporah and her husband, Pastor Isaac Kamau.

Mama Zipporah receiving a check from Diaspora Ministerial Conference in Geneva from former Vice President Moody Awori.

Mama Zipporah with her husband Isaac, their daughter Caroline Naiserian, and the children of Huruma Children's Home.

Mama Zipporah congratulating Mercy, a child at Huruma Children's Home, after winning a race.

Mirrium "Miracle" Njeri, healed of AIDS.

ORDINARY WOMAN, EXTRAORDINARY CALLING

❋

"The Lord knows how to rescue godly men from trials and to hold the unrighteous for the day of judgment."
—2 Peter 2:9

I N AUGUST OF 1996, my husband—who at the time was an Associate Pastor—and I were removed from our church. The community claimed that I was involved in satanic devil worship and spread rumors that I had given one of my daughters as an offering to the devil. They were determined to bring down my name, and did not hesitate to spread such foul lies. I know that the persecution my family suffered was a direct result of my former involvement in the Ngong Churches Huruma Project. The community desired to have me removed, simply because I had refused to misuse the funding. It was revenge, purely and simply. And while we were deeply hurt by the Church's words and actions, it did not cause us to waver in our faith.

Unfortunately, the time that these rumors began to spread was when my daughter was severely ill. The community used this to their advantage, and claimed that her illness was a result of the alleged devil offering I had made. Sadly, our church began to believe these rumors, and we were thus removed. And so we were left without a church, and Isaac had no desire to join another within a community that was causing us such great trouble.

The pain caused by the community's persecution was difficult for me to overcome; I spent much of my time in tears. Even as I rode the *matatu* (a local transit van), I could not stop the tears. But God spoke to me, even in my grief, and reminded me of a verse:

> *"For where two or three are assembled in my name, I am there among them."* —Matthew 18:20

The scripture makes no reference to the age or prestige of the individuals gathered together—it simply says two or three. I became filled with joy; you would have thought I had won a million dollars. But in fact, I had found something of even greater value.

I joined hands with my children and we began to pray. It was at this time that I asked my husband to continue preaching, and to become a pastor to our family. We did not have furniture during these services; all we had was a mat to sit upon. We had neither elders nor tithing members, but we had the spirit of the Lord. This was the beginning of what is today a healthy, thriving church. Now, there are over 150 members, most of whom are children entrusted to our care, but we have also gained support from the community. Now, many local individuals and international volunteers join us on Sunday to praise God within the Huruma Church.

The trials we underwent during this time strengthened our relationship with the Lord and caused us to draw closer to Him. Despite the persecution of the community and the resulting setbacks, my vision of a children's home burnt even stronger in my heart.

I had no desire to open a conventional orphanage—that was not the vision God had blessed me with. I never once toured a

Kenyan orphanage to serve as a basis for the Huruma Children's Home, choosing instead to begin with a clean slate. I had already determined that my children were not to be brought up in an orphanage; rather, they would be raised in a home environment, and grow up with daily biblical teachings.

God had placed this vision on me, an uneducated woman. And just as the apostle Paul had felt unworthy of his calling, so too did I. The thorn left in Paul's flesh was a reminder of his need to remain humble. Similarly, my lack of a proper education has continually humbled me.

"But He said to me, 'My grace is sufficient for you, for my power is made perfect in weakness.' Therefore I will boast all the more gladly about my weaknesses, so that Christ's power may rest on me. That is why, for Christ's sake, I delight in weaknesses, in insults, in hardships, in persecutions, in difficulties. For when I am weak, then I am strong."
—2 Corinthians 12:9–10

It is true; I was not worthy of the vision God had blessed me with. However, God's strength has been shown repeatedly through my weaknesses. I was put down, ridiculed, laughed at, and verbally abused. But despite the negative criticism and harsh judgments I received, I have endured in pursuing my God-given dream.

I asked my husband for the use of his land, in order that I could begin the children's home. Isaac took out a loan and we began to build a suitable home. At the time, we had only enough additional money to purchase tin for the roofing—we were left with no choice but to construct the building's foundation from mud.

I chose to single-handedly assemble our new mud home. Throughout the process my husband would come to observe me. I knew that he was questioning my sanity. After all, we had enjoyed a relatively good standard of life—we had a nice home in the city, and even a servant—but I now wanted to lower our class and give up our comforts. All for a house of mud.

Although it was never verbally expressed between us, I knew my husband thought I had gone mad, even as he helped to move our family into a mud hut. Through it all, he continued to stand by my side and support my vision. He had come to understand and respect my calling from God. Isaac loves to joke; however, he has always shown great respect toward me. In Kenya, this is a rare and precious thing. Many husbands continue to treat their wives like children, and most wives are looked down upon, misused and beaten. Unfortunately, this struggle for women to gain respect in society continues to this day. So I know that I am exceptionally blessed—even during a time when my husband questioned my sanity, he continued to support my vision and show respect.

In August 1990, my husband and I moved into the humble beginnings of our children's home. At the time, we had our three children, along with seven children left in my care from the Ngong Churches Huruma Project. The first structure was barely large enough to hold us; it was little more than a small mud hut, with cardboard partitions, a mud floor and tin roofing. The home had no electricity, no running water and no washroom facility—we used an outdoor pit toilet.

Living in a mud house such as this should have filled me with shame; instead, I was overjoyed. God had blessed me and allowed me to be content with our new standard of life. But while I knew I was pleased with our new way of living, I wanted to prove this fact to others. I wanted to show them that they could not bring me down. For this reason, I prayed that God would allow me to keep my large figure, which in Kenya is considered to be a sign of wealth and power. I also prayed that God would allow our children to continue receiving a good education; that growing up in a children's home would not set them back in any way. I was determined that, even though I had not had the opportunity to be properly educated, my children would. To this day I continue to stress the importance of education, for I do not want my children—currently numbered at over 150 —to be limited in any way.

Despite having done everything in my power to create a safe and protective children's home, I encountered a great deal of difficulty during my initial attempts to formally register the program. My proposal was denied on three separate occasions. Finally I became so distressed that I sat down with God and told Him that I had done everything I could—I had done everything required of me, continuing in my perseverance through any hardships, believing in faith that He would provide. I was very bold, telling God that *He* was the one who had failed; it was clear to me that I could not register the program myself. He had failed me and the children. I had already decided that I would continue to care for the children I had taken into my home; however, without registration as a children's home, I could no longer accept additional children. I would care for my current charges *and* be the best wife I could, but that is where it would have to end. I told God that, unless He provided, I could not continue with the project. I could not do it alone.

Three days after that, on October 14, 1990, I held in my hands the certificate for the Huruma Trust Fund. We were formally registered, and I praised God; this was the official beginning of the Huruma Children's Home. Through all this, I was reminded that it was not by any of my actions that the Home took form; rather, it was through God's. Not by my strength, but by His. Receiving

GIVING GOD WHAT IS
RIGHTFULLY HIS

W HEN HURUMA FORMALLY began, I was no longer employed, and we had little to no money with which to run a children's home. Initially, we could only provide our new family with one meal a day. At that time I was often so troubled and concerned for the children that I would frequently go to bed without taking anything to eat. I would often cry myself to sleep in desperation—the children deserved so much more than what I was able to provide.

On one particular Sunday, I had gone to Eldoret to visit my daughter Caroline, who was attending school there. As I was waiting for the evening train to come, I attended an evening service at a small church by the railway station. The message offered in the sermon was on the importance of tithing to God. And despite there being many within the congregation, I felt as though the pastor was speaking directly to me. Suddenly, I became the only one in the room. I knew that God was using him to speak to me, and I became ashamed of my actions. After all, God had given me and my family everything we had. I knew what I had to do.

I could not approach my husband about this matter; this was something just between God and me. I went home and took the two small bags of flour we had left, along with 400 Kenyan shillings (about $5.70). I wrapped the flour up in a table cloth and stuffed the money into my bra; I did not want my husband to know I was tithing all we had left. I headed toward the church and left everything we had left, as a gift to God. It was a big sacrifice for me to make; I had no idea how we were going to feed the children, and I had no choice but to beg for bread on my way home from the church.

But God blessed my family. By the time I returned home I was greeted by a woman who blessed Huruma with significant support; soon after, we also received one of our first corporate sponsors, Barclays Bank. By tithing all we had left, I had taken a step forward in faith. I trusted that God would provide for our needs, and He most certainly did.

Some would think me foolish for tithing everything we had. But in my heart, I knew it was what God required of me. I took a step forward in faith, trusting that God would provide, and I praised His name; our needs did not go unnoticed or unmet.

BITTERNESS IS A BITTER ROOT

I N 1991, I had the opportunity to travel back to the United States—this time, to Florida. Again, the trip itself is not what I remember; rather, it was the way in which God spoke to me that drastically influenced my life. He revealed to me that "bitterness is a bitter root"; this was the important message that touched my heart and soul. The message was delivered by a woman who had suffered a severe diving accident. She had completely lost the use of her arms, but had learned to write with her feet. After her accident she had many who prayed for her, but no healing came upon her body. I thought of my own struggles with illness, my heart condition and God's miraculous grace that came upon my life and healed me.

The woman's love for God was deep. She did not blame any-one for what happened to her, nor did she allow herself to be controlled by bitterness. Her faith and her fortitude inspired me. I began to realize just how much resentment had built up within me. There were many, back within the Kenyan community, who I had not yet forgiven. They had deeply hurt me and had done their best to bring shame to my name. But it was only once I was far from home that I realized: God wanted me to forgive. In fact, He demands that we forgive: "If a brother wrongs you seven times, forgive seven times a day." I, too, had to forgive those who had previously done me wrong. I had to let go; surrendering the past to God and refusing to allow bitterness to control my life.

I don't understand why God chooses to speak to me so much while I am abroad, but I praise God for revealing something of such great importance to me. It took a trip to the United States and the testimony of one woman for me to realize that things in my life were in need of change. My perspective had to change. Forgiveness was necessary. I chose to push away the bitterness and forgive those who had wronged me, and upon returning home I felt a great sense of relief. While many of the individuals continued to show bitterness and resentment toward me, with God's strength I was able to forgive them of their actions and move forward with my life.

✳✳✳✳✳✳✳

Shortly after my return to Kenya, several men that were praying in the local mountains came with a message for me. I had never met or even heard of these men; however, it seemed they knew of me. They told me that God had sent them; God had told them of Zipporah Kamau, and had given them an important message to deliver to her: God has healed her son from a heart condition.

Since he was born, my son George had not been a healthy baby, and he did not thrive in his environment. It seemed like we spent every other day with him in one hospital after another, whether for chest congestion or trouble breathing. The doctors couldn't tell us what was wrong with him, and his condition continued to worsen. In desperation, I took him to see a doctor I knew from Ngong, who inspected George thoroughly before recommending he be x-rayed. When the results came back that my son had a hole in his heart, I was so shocked I could hardly speak. I went home that day in a daze, wondering over and over again why God would have allowed my son to be born so sickly.

I was at a loss for what to do, and feared for my son's life. Prayer was the only treatment option available to us.

So it was with equal parts surprise and joy that I greeted the news brought to me by the men from the mountains. As I said, I had never before met or even heard of these men. They did not come looking for money, nor did they once ask me for a single thing. They expected nothing in return and disappeared as quickly as they came. The entire purpose of their trip was to tell me of the healing God had provided for my son. But what they said was true: never again has my son struggled with such severe health problems. I praise God, for his heart had been healed. I had borne witness to a miracle.

I cannot say for certain why God brought this miracle upon our family. However, I personally believe that God chose to bless me because of the persecution I underwent, the faith I held firm to, and the forgiveness I extended to those who had brought harm to me. I praise God for the healing he brought to my son, and I am eternally thankful for His blessings.

CHEATED

"You have not lied to me but to God."
—Acts 5:4

W HEN DIRECTING A children's home, many needs arise
that require significant financial support. As the demands
of the home were already beginning to grow, I was thrilled to
hear of an organization willing to help raise financial support for
Huruma. I soon received an invitation to enter into partnership
with them. After happily accepting, they arranged to fly me to
the United States, and they organized a busy schedule that would
allow me to speak to many church groups and organizations regarding the Huruma Children's Home.

It was during one of these many speaking opportunities that
I was approached by a lady interested in helping our cause. With
great excitement, she began to tell me of a donation she had
made to the Huruma Children's Home. God, she said, had put
our needs on her heart, and she was led to provide a significant
amount of financial funding. The woman was extremely generous, and I could sense she had a great love for God. But while
I knew she spoke the truth, I also knew that I had not received
any donation in the substantial amount she described. In fact, the
total amount of *all* the donations I had received was significantly
less than the amount she specified.

This was how God chose to reveal a serious issue to me.

I may not be an educated woman; however, God has seen fit to bless me with the wisdom necessary to properly direct the Huruma Children's Home, as well as efficiently manage the Huruma Trust Fund that supports it. As a Christian, I had assumed the best of my fellow brother-in-faith, my gracious financial partner. But unfortunately, my faith in a Christian organization was misused; I was being taken advantage of.

Their invitation for partnership was very clear and straightforward—they offered to help me raise support for the Huruma Children's Home, without any caveats. Throughout all our correspondence, they never once mentioned that I would only be receiving a small portion of the funding generated through my speaking opportunities; I have kept a record of all correspondence proving this fact. But most troubling of all, the individuals attending the arranged meetings were misinformed as well: even those who felt led to donate funding were doing so under the impression that it would be going directly to the Huruma Children's Home.

On the contrary: we received less than 25 percent of the money raised. The vast majority of funding received through my speaking was directed elsewhere.

The situation reminded me of the biblical story of Ananias and Sapphira, found in Acts 5:1–11. In those days, no one went without; everyone who had something to give would share it with those in need. Ananias and Sapphira had much wealth in the land they owned, and upon selling it, they held back a portion of money to keep for themselves—very similar to the portion held back by this organization. Ananias and Sapphira approached the apostle Paul and gave him a fragment of the money, to share among those in need. But their hearts were not pure. They claimed to give everything they had, yet they withheld most of their money. Paul was furious with their lie and explained to them: "You have not lied to me, but to God." (Acts 5:4)

The organization withheld information from me and knowingly perpetuated a lie. And what is worse, it was not me they lied to, but God. I had no choice but to terminate the relationship, for I must keep my actions accountable to God in all things; I could no longer be a part of such deception. They assumed that I would not understand the contract, and thought they could take advantage of me. But what troubles me most is that the individuals inspired to give were misled as well.

Upon confronting key members of the organization, I was even more disturbed to find that they had no intention of bringing the matter before their board of directors. Rather, they wanted to resolve my concerns privately, which inspired an even greater concern in me. If there was no wrongdoing in their actions, they would not have protested so strongly against making the matter public and putting the question before their board.

Adding further insult, the organization falsely accused me of holding back money for my own personal gain, rather than for the use they specified. To this day, I do not understand where this accusation came from; however, I keep peace in my heart, for God knows the truth. He knows of the many personal sacrifices I have made on behalf of my children's well-being. He knows the desires of my heart, and sees how I have chosen to live alongside the children; I am in no better position than they, for we share the same standard of living.

When God puts a vision in your heart, you can be certain that Satan will do his best to deter you from your calling. And although I had not expected to encounter such a trial from fellow believers, I remained true to the vision God has blessed me with. I knew that I would be held accountable for my actions, and I could not in good faith associate with such corruption and deception.

God would deal with them.

LESSONS ABROAD

I T WAS DURING a trip to Indiana in the United States that
God again provided for me. The trip was designed to raise
funds and support for the Huruma Children's Home; however,
during my travels I had the opportunity to visit with a woman
who was originally from Kenya. I had known her father, it turned
out; he was an elder of the Church and a well-respected man.
His daughter, however, struggled with a drinking problem and
did not have a personal relationship with the Lord. I had been
told not to visit her, but chose to go despite the warnings. I had
no idea what I would speak to her about, but as I was greeted by
her husband and began a conversation with him, I found myself
naturally speaking of my ministry back in Kenya. It was at this
point that the woman took great interest. She came close and sat
beside me as I continued to speak. I praise God, for our conversation led her to accept the Lord as her personal savior and turn
away from her past wrongdoings.

I could not stay with her long, though; I had another meeting I was to attend to. The two of us shared a warm good-bye,
and I entered the cab waiting for me. Unfortunately, along the
way the taxi driver became lost, and by the time he found the
location, the individuals I had agreed to meet with had already
left. I was lost with only twenty dollars to my name, and I still
had to pay the cab driver. I asked the driver to take me back to
the bus station.

It was here at the station that I laid out my luggage and slept on top of them for the night. I can only imagine how foolish I looked. But despite being alone in a foreign country, lost and without assistance, I had great peace in my heart. I had no fears or concerns, for I knew that my Lord was going to provide for me. Most would think I was acting senselessly, but it was in faith that I returned to the station and rested there for the night.

My faith was not misplaced. God is always looking after my best interests, and the very next morning, a complete stranger approached me and left me with a large sum of money.

It turned out that the woman who had just the day before received the Lord into her life—the very one I had been told not to visit—had been given divine wisdom from God. During the night, God revealed to her in a dream that I was in desperate need of assistance. The following morning she sent a friend to the station with money, and gave her specific instructions to find the woman from Kenya in need of aid and leave the money with her.

Upon receiving the financial support guided to me by God, I was able to continue on with my meetings and raise much needed funding for the Huruma Children's Home.

Lesson learned?

WATER PROBLEMS

I T WAS DURING the time of El Niño that we at Huruma ran out of water. It was not uncommon for us to encounter a problem with our well, but now we had completely run dry—there was no water to drink, no water to cook with, and no water to clean with. Often we were forced to purchase our water, and when the money was not available, we had to scavenge.

The land my husband purchased was in the Ngong Hills, and as such we were far from any water source. When the money was available, we were able to purchase water from a nearby town, but we did not always have the available finances. Many times we had no choice but to walk a great distance to Nairobi with our five-liter cans to scavenge for water.

Here in Kenya, and especially in Nairobi, typhoid is a serious problem; many have died due to contaminated water. The water we were able to bring back was no exception—it was so dirty that it was not even suitable for animals to consume. But we had no other option. I became greatly concerned for the health and well-being of the children I had been entrusted with, and so I prayed to God and asked him to put His hand of protection upon my children, so that not a single child would become ill from consuming such unsuitable water. Our water shortage continued for *ten years,* but praise God, my children did not become ill.

Unfortunately, this was also during a time when I was suffering from many false accusations, including one that said I was abusing the children in my care. During one of our water excursions, it happened that one of the boys in my care accidentally fell and broke his arm. It was an unfortunate accident; however, from that moment on, I decided that we would no longer scavenge for water. I told God that He had to provide water for the children; He had to help me dig a well. My first attempt was unsuccessful; although I had dug down so far that you could no longer see the end of the well, as soon as we found water, the well caved in. But to our good fortune, God provided us with a large tractor that was able to successfully find water. God provided for us.

LOST COWS AND FOUND
FORGIVENESS

※※※

"A thief must certainly make restitution."
—Exodus 22:3

ONE MORNING, I awoke to the sad news that two cows
had gone missing from the Huruma property overnight.
I did not understand why God would allow for such a thing to
happen. As my husband attempted to calm me, all I could say
was, "I want the children to have their cows back!" I asked God,
"Why?" I simply could not understand.

The children of Huruma depended on the cows' milk in order to make sure that they received the proper nutrition—this
was the only source of calcium we could afford to provide. I had
a hard time understanding how anyone could steal from children,
and an even harder time understanding why God would allow
such a thing to happen in the first place. I pondered this all morning, until I finally approached a good friend with my troubles.

Her response was simple: she asked if I had prayed to God
concerning the matter. It is during such times of distress that it
is all too easy to overlook the importance of prayer. This, unfortunately, was one of those moments. We joined hands and
proceeded to pray together: "God, those two cows belonged to
the children. Bring them back." And that was that.

Later that day, I was reading an article on forgiveness I had found within a Kenyan Christian magazine. By pure coincidence, the situation it described was one similar to mine: a man had been stolen from; however, he understood the importance of forgiveness and, upon receiving back his stolen property, he immediately forgave the thief. The article explained the importance of forgiving those who have wronged you and led me to wonder if I would be able to forgive the one who had stolen our cows. I knew it was possible; be that as it may, I still wanted them returned.

It was not long after this that a community neighbor approached me and explained that he had seen a cow that looked like ours in the nearby slaughterhouse. Upon hearing this, I left immediately and found that one of the cows had already been sold at the market; however, the man who had purchased it began to feel ill the moment he took possession. He followed the thieves who had sold him the cow back into the forest to ask for the return of his money—he knew there was something wrong with the purchase he had made, and he no longer wanted to keep the cow.

It was shortly after this confrontation that the police arrived, as did I. The moment I saw the children's cow she let out a squeal. Just imagine a cow squealing; if I had not heard it for myself, I would not have believed it was possible. I became so overwhelmed with joy that I actually ran up to it, wrapped my arms around its neck, and stood there, just hugging the cow. I know I appeared foolish; I truly didn't care. I was thrilled to have found one of the children's cows.

Unfortunately, the thieves still had to admit to what they had done. As I'm sure you can imagine, they were hesitant to speak of their crime in front of the police; however, I explained to them that if both of the children's cows were returned, I would truly forgive them of their wrong.

They were reluctant to believe me; too often people make false claims when trying to persuade another individual. But I reassured them that I had made a promise to God: if both cows were returned safely, I would forgive whoever had taken them. The two thieves openly admitted to taking the cows from the Huruma property, and the police proceeded to severely beat the thieves. I intervened, demanding that the police stop; for if both of the children's cows were returned, I was prepared to forgive the men of their wrong.

I thank God, for that very night both cows were returned safely to their pen. And I praise God, for one of the men who stole from the children was led to the Lord that very day. I began to understand why God had permitted the children's cows to be taken; it was only for a short time—just long enough for a man to become Christian and repent his ways. I was reminded that, while we do not always know the will of the Lord, He is always looking after us.

In my heart, I truly did forgive the thieves, and I praise God for the unique way in which He chose to bring this man to the knowledge of His saving grace. To this very day, the man continues to refer to himself in Kiswahili as *Mali Ya Mungu*—"stealer from God."

BETWEEN INTUITION AND FAITH

B EING THE DIRECTOR of a trust fund *and* mother to over
150 children demands more hours than are in a day, let
alone what time I have available. Daily problems and concerns
arise that require both careful wisdom and quick solutions. I have
come to rely upon God's direction and guidance for the frequent
decisions I must make. I am fortunate in this, for God has blessed
me with a strong gift of intuition; God often chooses to reveal
unseen problems and their solutions to me through my dreams.

Many people, those who do not understand the power of
God or His ability to guide an individual, have questioned my
approach to solving problems. They instead have doubted me,
and in doing so, have doubted God's power. I have had to remain
strong in my faith in God, and trust that He will reveal to me all
that I need to know, as well as providing me with the wisdom
needed to handle any situations that arise.

One such situation occurred when a new teacher was employed to educate the children at Huruma. At first, all seemed
well; but upon her joining our organization, I began to have severe
pains in my chest. At first I simply wrote it off as heartburn, and
considered it to be a minor illness. But the pain persisted, and I
began to wonder whether there weren't some other, hidden cause.

The teacher made mention that she was able to lead in worship. As we wanted to fully utilize her skills, we asked if she would
join us and help lead our worship music during our Church

services. But unfortunately we found that she was unable to sing along or lead in any way. She accused us of worshiping wrong, and we left it at that.

And still the pains in my chest continued. I soon began to associate these pains with the presence of our new teacher; for it was only in her presence that I became ill. I took the matter to God and sought after His guidance. In this way, I was led to believe that our new teacher was involved in satanic devil worship and was therefore clearly not suitable to educate our children.

I had no choice but to approach the teacher herself concerning this matter. My God-given intuition was correct: she admitted that she was involved with a group of individuals she should not have been associating with. She further confessed that she had been actively participating in satanic devil worship along with these individuals. Despite this, we decided to give her a second chance, and allow her to remain employed—provided, of course, that she changed her ways.

Unfortunately, my pains did not cease. During one particular Church service, I felt uneasy, as though a new presence had entered the room. Yet when I opened my eyes I saw that nothing had changed. However, just as God has blessed me with many gifts, so He has also blessed one of my children. During worship, one of the children saw a dark figure enter the room. His face was menacing; my son described him as violently sticking out his tongue, all the while seated just beside the teacher. Just imagine: a demon entering God's house of prayer. I knew that the new teacher was the cause of the troubles we were facing. God guided me and helped me to realize that she needed to be removed from the Huruma Children's Home.

As my husband Isaac and I went to her to relieve her of her duties, I warned him that this was a serious matter, and that it should not be taken lightly. She greeted us by praising God, but again the pains in my chest continued. I could not bring myself to shake her hand; my hands remained behind my back as I told her simply that I was fine. My husband, however, did not heed the advice I had given him; he did not see the seriousness of the matter. But even as he went to shake her hand, right before their hands met—*whoosh*—his trousers fell to the floor. Just like that, God was able to prevent even Isaac from greeting this woman. I am relieved to say that she is no longer employed here at Huruma, and that consequently my chest pains have come to an end.

Were it not for the help and guidance that God continues to provide me with, I know that I would not be able to properly manage the Huruma Children's Home. I must continually rely on the intuition with which God has blessed me, and have faith that God will direct me to where I need to go. It is not easy to explain my actions to those who do not place faith in God.

But I hate to think of the troubles this organization would encounter were it not for His guidance.

GOD'S WATCHMEN

❧

I T WAS IN August of 2005 that I felt the need to employ a
night watchman to secure the Huruma Children's Home
property. While we are a gated community that is locked down
after sunset, there are still many ways for thieves to gain access
to our property. Violent theft and robbery is a significant problem here in Kenya. Upon looking over all the many generous
donations God had blessed us with, I began to realize that we
had quickly become a target. What is more, several individuals
within the community were unhappy with our success and
jealous of the support we had been receiving. This put my
family's life at risk.

I set out to find a watchman of Godly character to secure our
property during the evenings. Upon review of a list of potential
employees, I came across one particular man of interest. He had
extraordinary strength and liked to brag about having tossed a
cow out of his way. The very thought of this seemed absurd;
however, he truly was known for his strength, which was exactly
what we needed.

During the interview process, I explained our need for proper
security to protect the staff and children. But throughout the
entire time I was speaking, the man had a puzzled look on his
face. Finally he asked, "Mama Zipporah, what happened to all the
other watchmen you hired?"

I had no idea what he was talking about; I had only recently realized the need for a night watchmen, and so had hired no one before this time. So I asked him to explain further.

"The watchmen that carry torches and guard your property at night—there were many of them."

I still had no idea what he was talking about. We had never before employed a watchman at Huruma, and we definitely could not afford to employ multiple watchmen with torches to guard the property. After I completed the interview and the man left my office, all I could do was laugh. Watchmen with torches, guarding the Huruma property! Imagine that...

But then I began to imagine a security system as designed by God—an army of angels, protecting our property and guarding the children's lives. Each one bearing a torch—the light of God.

The man I had interviewed was very sure of what he had seen. He had truly wanted to know what had happened to the many torch-bearing watchmen guarding Huruma. I have since heard of accounts from missionaries who entered the areas belonging to remote tribes in Africa, describing instances when villagers had set out during the evening to attack their huts, only to be confronted by glowing guards, each with a drawn sword.

God sends angels to protect the lives of His servants. I have come to believe that it was God that had provided protection for the children here at Huruma—the protection of torch-bearing angels.

My husband was not so quick to believe. He questioned the sanity of the man I had interviewed, and wrote off the situation. But several months after the interview, a well-respected man within the community approached my husband. He wanted to know where Huruma had found the funds necessary to purchase the bows and arrows for the watchmen we had guarding the property each evening. My husband was speechless; he did not have an answer for the gentlemen he was speaking to. You must understand the rarity of a situation like this: my husband is seldom speechless and invariably has an answer. But praise God, for he too has come to believe.

While we have been very fortunate here at Huruma, many of our employees have come across difficulties. The majority of our employees are housed away from the Huruma property, and in October of that same year, trouble came upon them.

Violent men within the community had gained word that employees of the Huruma Children's Home had just received pay. Sadly, we know from this that these men had received inside information. Huruma employees are faith-based; we are only able to pay our teachers and aides when money is available through donations. Huruma employees are known not to receive regular wages, and never encounter trouble during the months we are unable to pay. But the night following payday, several teachers and staff members were raided by forceful thieves demanding money.

The thieves approached various teachers individually in their sleep. They demanded they be quiet, and instructed the teachers to hand over their money. Sadly Pamala, the third teacher they attacked, was a deaf woman, employed to assist us in educating a hearing-impaired child. When the thieves approached her, she could not therefore hear their demands. Further, as it was dark, she was unable to read their lips. She did not hear them tell her to be quiet, nor did she hear their demands for money. As she helplessly curled herself into a ball, they continued to beat and stab her, demanding she be quiet and hand over her money. All the while, her young son looked on from a dark corner of the room. Imagine the horror: watching helplessly as your mother is beaten.

Pamala's screams and cries were loud enough to wake the other teachers, causing the three thieves to flee. They had escaped with the salaries of three teachers, but only after they had also caused serious harm to several individuals.

It was three o'clock in the morning when we rushed several Huruma employees to receive emergency medical care. Pamala was kept overnight in order to stitch up her many cuts; even then, she had no idea why she had been beaten. Her son, clueless himself, has been left with the terrifying memory of that night.

Unfortunately, the thieves visited more than just the teachers' homes. A married couple employed here at Huruma was also attacked. During the robbery, all the wife could do was scream, "Please do not kill my husband; if you do, kill me as well." Thankfully, once their entire monthly salary—the only money they had to live on—had been handed over, the thieves had no desire to cause additional harm and fled the scene.

Despite the troubles of the evening, all Huruma staff members and children joined together early in the morning to worship God. Together as a family, we praised the Lord and thanked Him for saving the lives of those employed here at Huruma. I praise God, for this incident of horror could have been much worse. Fortunately, the thieves were caught and prosecuted for the crimes they had committed. And another blessing: the incident also reunited Pamala with her family, with whom she had not been in contact for many years. They were proud that, even at a time when the Kenyan unemployment rate hovered around 50 percent, their disabled daughter was able to hold a good job.

God continues to work in ways that go far beyond my understanding; however, I know that everything occurs for a reason, and I trust that God is continuously looking after our needs.

FINANCIAL NEEDS

W E ARE CURRENTLY unable to provide education for our high school students here at Huruma, so once our children graduate from junior high we transfer them to another educational facility. Some of our youths are currently attending boarding schools, while others have stayed local. The transfer they receive depends upon the grades they've achieved. In faith, Huruma provides funding for their education through donations received.

It was during a school board meeting that I was contacted by one of the schools being attended by several Huruma youths. I was informed that, if I could not pay their tuition immediately, the Huruma youths would be expelled from the school. Unfortunately, last we had checked, the Huruma Trust Fund account did not have enough money to even purchase detergent for the children to clean their clothes. But acting in faith, I told the school representative to come and pick up a check.

Immediately after ending the phone conversation, all I could do was laugh and exclaim, "Oh God, help me!"

In Kenya, it is considered a criminal offence for any individual to write a check when their account funds are insufficient. This crime is not taken lightly; anyone reported will receive three years in jail. I had no idea what would happen to the Huruma Children's Home if I were to be jailed for three years. I had taken a risk, yes, but I remained faithful that God would provide. I truly believe, as I have always believed, in the importance of education. These children have already had a rough start in life; I believe that education plays an important role in helping them develop. I did not want our youths to be removed from the educational institution.

A representative from the high school arrived, and I unhesitatingly handed him a large check to cover the tuition fees for five Huruma youths.

The very next day we received a small amount of money from volunteers who were staying with us at the time. As my husband went to deposit the funds, he also happened to check the balance of the Huruma Trust Fund. I praise God, for He had provided for us; we had received a very large donation. We did not need to worry about there not being enough funds within our account, and I did not need to worry about being jailed!

NGAI

THERE HAVE BEEN many times when God has placed deathly ill children within my care. As I do not wish to see the death of even a single child, I have asked God to put His healing protection on Huruma. I cannot even begin to tell you how many times I have witnessed God perform healing miracles within our family. We have been blessed to witness God's hand actively at work within our lives.

Joyce Wangari came to us in November 2005. As she was in the final stage of AIDS, she had been turned away from the hospital. The doctors told her family to take her home—there was nothing more they could do for her.

Joyce's mother had struggled against the disease for some time. Before her mother's death, Joyce, with a great heart of compassion, took concern over her mother and tended to her wounds. Family members believe that it was during this time that she herself contracted HIV.

Joyce and her brothers were sent to live with their grandmother after the death of their mother. Unfortunately, the grandmother was elderly and poor; she was barely able to meet her needs, let alone the needs of her grandchildren. Once they realized that Joyce was HIV positive, there was nothing that could be done. The grandmother was unable to afford medication. And, due to a lack of education, the family did not see the value behind antiretroviral drugs. Without medication, Joyce's condition quickly worsened and she was left in the hospital.

It was after being released from the hospital that Huruma became involved. After Joyce was removed from medical attention and the family was told that she would not survive, the grandmother lost hope. She did not have the financial resources to properly care for the children. Thankfully, an uncle had come to hear of Huruma and decided to bring the children to us.

When he approached me regarding their condition, it was at a time when Joyce was exceptionally ill. She was frail and unable to walk on her own, even with support. It was a struggle for her to get anywhere. Joyce had lost control of her bladder and had several large, open flesh wounds where—even before death—her body had begun to rot.

Just looking at her and the suffering she was undergoing at such a young age was enough to make even the hardest heart cry out. I accepted both Joyce and her two brothers without hesitation.

For health reasons, Joyce was given separate sleeping quarters from the other children; her brother, however, was fully integrated into the Huruma home and immediately began attending classes in the school. I thank God for the staffing team I have been blessed with. Several workers were willing to clean Joyce, an older girl took on the responsibility of washing her clothes, and both I and an international volunteer tended to her wounds. Many took an active role in providing care for her and making her life comfortable.

Joyce immediately began receiving antiretroviral drugs to boost her immune system, and we began to provide her with adequate nutrition. Gradually we began to see a positive change.

With support, she was able to begin walking. I wanted to see God perform another miracle; I wanted to see Joyce fully recovered.

I held on to this hope. Over time, Joyce began to regain strength. She was able to walk herself to the washroom and feed herself. She even began to calculate sums and perform basic multiplication. Slowly, and with unsteady hand writing, she could print out her name. Were it not for AIDS, Joyce would have been entering Grade 9—she enjoyed school and truly excelled at mathematics.

On one particularly good day, Joyce made her way outside to sit in the sun. As she enjoyed the fresh air she began to laugh and cry out to God, shouting, "Ngai" in her native Kikuyu language. This continued for hours, but we were still a bit skeptical of her condition. She told one teacher that a car was coming to pick her up. This was the happiest moment of her final days.

The very next morning, Joyce suffered a seizure and went into a coma. Upon taking her to the hospital, it was discovered that she had meningitis and she was kept overnight for observation. Grieved by the news, we returned home to update the children on her status. The very next day Ryan, one of our little babies, experienced a seizure. After he was rushed to the hospital, it was discovered to be another case of meningitis. Everyone had to be treated to prevent further outbreak, but thankfully no other case arose.

However, Joyce was never able to recover.

I was reminded of a dream one of my older girls had shared with me. The previous night, this girl dreamed that Joyce was crying out in the middle of the night for help; however, she did not do anything about it. The next morning, when everyone awoke to find that Joyce had passed away, this girl felt terrible that she did not wake me up the night before to tell me of Joyce's cries. In the dream, I refused to accept the death, and continued to cradle Joyce's limp body in my arms. After hearing of this dream, I did not want to accept the warning.

Following Joyce's death, Huruma began to experience a significant financial burden. I had many pressing bills to pay, and had only 200 shillings (approximately $2.80) in the Huruma account. We also had yet to make arrangements for Joyce's funeral.

In running the Home, I have learned that funding is based on faith. I don't ask for money. I trust in God. And so in this case, I did not send out an urgent email explaining the situation to my supporters. Rather, I prayed and trusted in faith that God would provide.

I am grateful that God gave me the opportunity to learn from Joyce. Even during great pain and suffering, she continued to trust in God and call out His name. It is my prayer that, as the Huruma clinic begins to expand and grow, we may be able to accept more children that have been turned away from hospitals, and even from other children's homes. I pray that God will use Huruma to bring hope to ill children and restore them back to health.

CONCLUSION

❖

"People talk of the sacrifice I have made in spending so much time in Africa. Can that be called a sacrifice which is simply paying back a small part of a great debt owing to our God which we can never repay? Is that a sacrifice which brings its own best reward in healthful activity, the consciousness of doing good, peace of mind, and a bright hope of glorious destiny hereafter? Away with the word in such a view and with such a thought. It is emphatically no sacrifice. Say, rather it is a privilege." —David Livingstone, quoted in *Profiles in Faith*

WITHIN MY LIFE, serving God has been both a blessing and privilege. As people speak of the supposed sacrifices I have made, I find I can relate to David Livingstone's words—my life has truly been without sacrifice. Livingstone's time as a missionary in Africa sets forth a good example for each of our lives. Nothing we do can ever pay our debt to the Lord in full. There is no sacrifice in doing what God has called us to do; we simply need to cling to our faith.

Unfortunately, too many individuals in today's modern society lack faith. They have either been persuaded not to believe in God, or have been taught that God is not capable of performing miracles. Throughout the Bible we can read countless examples of miracles being performed by either Jesus or by one of His disciples. However, these miracles were performed by individuals of great faith, and were performed on those who had faith themselves. They saw the miracles of God and came to believe.

We have been blessed with countless international volunteers who have come to Africa to humbly offer their time. Unfortunately, not all volunteers are willing to humble themselves, nor do they all have a personal relationship with the Lord. But we have accepted this as an opportunity to evangelize and teach individuals from around the world the Gospel. I remember one volunteer in particular: they had come to us without a relationship with the Lord, and were unwilling to accept Kenyan traditions. They were insistent that they knew what was best, and at times it was difficult to deal with this individual; I could see the empty void in their life. Their self-righteous attitude was at times hard to bear; however, we continued to demonstrate the love of God and gradually we noticed a change in their behavior. But even then, we did not realize how dramatic a change the individual had undergone.

It was not until their final day, when reflecting on their experience at Huruma, when they spoke in front of the Home. The individuals explained that they had come with an empty void in their life, and that they had been searching for something, yet did not know what it was they were searching for. Finally, within Huruma, the individuals had come to realize that what was missing in their life was faith. With tears streaming down their faces, they explained that they had never before been surrounded by so many believers strong in faith. Never before had this individual experienced such great faith; and for them, it was a life changing faith that led them to God.

"Because you have seen me, you have believed; blessed are those who have not seen and yet have believed."
—John 20:29

Picture wind: it is not visible to the human eye, yet no rational person will argue that wind does not exist. You cannot see it; yet you are able to experience its effects. You can feel how a cool breeze brings relief on a hot summer day; you can see how the wind shakes branches and picks up dust. The same is true with God. You do not see Him, but through faith you can experience all that God is capable of.

Faith in God is not something you can see, but my testimony is living proof that faith in God is something you can experience; you can witness the result of faith in the world. For, even if you only have faith the size of a mustard seed, you are enabling God to perform miraculous wonders in your life. I have come to realize, through life and experience and through God's word, that the size of my faith affects what God is capable of doing within my life. I truly believe that God will provide, and He has done just that.

To believe in God's capabilities is to have faith. I have put my faith in God, and in doing so, I have come to realize the calling He intended for my life. I have faith that God will continue to assist me in ministering to the children entrusted to my care. I know that God is real, active, and present in my daily life.

"When a man's ways are pleasing to the Lord, he makes even his enemies live at peace with him." —Proverbs 16:7

Every day, needs arise that I cannot fill. Children are turned away due to lack of room; even food becomes scarce at times. But I continue to praise God and remain faithful, for in His time our needs are met.

Despite our many needs God has never let us truly go without.

It is hard for me to understand why God would choose to use a woman of limited education. But use me He has. My life is a testimony of faith, for as it is written in Matthew 17:20–21, "I tell you the truth, if you have faith as small as a mustard seed, you can say to this mountain: 'Move from here to there,' and it will move. Nothing will be impossible for you."

I put my faith in God. He has chosen me to be a mother to the motherless, and for that, I trust that He will provide.

> *"Faith is being sure of what we hope for and certain of what we do not see."*—Hebrews 11:1

MOTIVATION FROM HURUMA

Children's Stories

I T CAN BE argued that an adult's identity is synonymous with their career choice; in other words, their employment defines their very self-being. But there are many who go through life, viewing their career choice as nothing more than a meaningless chore. They would likely be offended if you were to state that their job defines who they are. I am certain their lives could successfully disprove the theological link between one's employment and one's identity.

But then there are the fortunate few, those whose work comes without drudgery. For them, work is embraced as a defining contribution to their very self. It is part of them. I am one of the blessed individuals whose identity has become affiliated with their vocational choice. I love what I do. My work has shaped who I am.

And it must be said that my children have unknowingly affected my identity as well. In order to truly understand the motivation behind my life, it is imperative that you are introduced to the children. You must understand how they have come to Huruma, each arriving with a unique history they must overcome. My life, my identity, is too closely tied to these children for their stories to go untold. As I share in both their joys and sorrows, they have become a contributing influence that has shaped my life.

But my children's pasts are not for me to publish. Rather, with their willingness and permission, it is my desire for several Huruma children to share their testimonies personally. I want you to read, in their own words, about their lives.

Zipporah

Zipporah was rescued from her stepfather by police in 2000. Her mother was married to a Muslim and he was very strict. One day, when she was only six years old, she went with other children to their home. When the father came to know about it, he beat her badly and later tied her legs and her hands together, and hung her in a tree for two days without water or food. When she was untied, the ropes had already damaged her hands and legs, and she had deep wounds in both her hands.

When the surrounding neighbors noticed that they had not seen her for some days, they reported the matter to the police, saying she must have been killed. Immediately, the police responded and went to search the house, where they found Zipporah huddled in the corner, in a lot of pain. They took her out of the house and brought Zipporah to our home. The parents were taken to court, but because her mother chose to protect her husband and refused to testify, the stepfather was let go. Zipporah was badly hurt by this. She asked us, "Why did my mother choose to protect my stepfather when he almost killed me?"

Today, Zipporah has finished Grade 12 and is enrolled at university in Uganda. Our thanks go out to her sponsors, Mr. and Mrs. David Hutchmen, who have supported her like she was their own daughter.

George Laiyan

The orphanage (my home) was started while I was young, (5 years old) and I found it normal to have so many brothers and sisters around. It was a good time for me when I was young, because I had friends to play with all the time. We even shared food, clothing, and sleeping places with the children and I was happy to be around them, and we were happy when we were together. When I went to high school, I used to miss home so much, and I was homesick most of the time. When I went to university I made sure that most weekends I was at home, because I missed the company of the children. To me, Huruma is my home and I love it so much and am thankful to my mom, Mama Zipporah, for having a bottomless heart filled with love, compassion, and mercy toward the orphaned and destitute, and in helping them achieve their goals. Lastly, I thank the Almighty God for creating Mama and giving her lots of strength, love, and compassion to help children, and also for having the best family in the world: Isaac, Zipporah, Caroline, Catherine, I love you very much. You are the greatest gifts God gave me. Thank you for everything.

Ben Sakali

Dear mom,

I am thankful for what you have done in my life. I was a man gone astray, lost; but I thank you, for you have rescued me and given me a second chance. I kept on thinking I would be a failure throughout my life, but I kept on, knowing that failure is not fatal, and that it is success that counts.

My worst life experience was when I was away from Huruma for a number of years. Surely I was like a sheep lost by its shepherd. In my experience, I would hate to see any of my siblings go through this kind of hardship. You are the greatest gift I have ever had in this life and I am who I am today because of you. I am thankful that you took part as my mother and ensured that my school debt was fully settled. I used to depend on the volunteers, but once they were gone and out of sight, I thought that would be the end of my life. I could not be allowed back to school until I cleared my school balance.

I lack the exact words to express my feeling of thanks to you, but I ask God to bless you and grant you countless years to devote yourself to loving and helping the needy. I promise to do my best and to never let tears roll down your cheeks because of me, but I will be making you smile instead. I promise to do well academically and improve on my school grades. I know I am capable of being prosperous in life, if only I prepare for it now using the available resources that God has given me.

Though your hard work is not recognized by your fellow Kenyans, God has a reward for you and does know what you are going through. You might not have received a Nobel Prize to show your life achievements, but it awaits in God's hands. I can't wait to celebrate your success in life.

From,
Ben

Susan
My name is Susan Nadupoi. I am the second born in a family of seven children. I am from the Masaai community from a place known as Oloshoibor just behind the Ngong Hills, where we lived as a family with my mother and Dad (who was my stepfather). I didn't live a good life despite the fact that I had a mum because I used to not go to school, though my sister and brothers were in school by then. It was not my mother's will for me never to go to school, but my stepdad did not want me to

get an education. My mum tried all she could do to take me to school, but it was all in vain.

My mother had no option but to let me stay at home, doing nothing. It was not as though just staying at home was enjoyable; I was thoroughly beaten by my stepfather, often with no reason. When my mother questioned him about the brutal beatings, he would say that I was disrespectful to him. There came a time where he would go drink and when he came back home he would beat up my mum and he would throw us out of the house. It was very hard for my mum to explain to me about the hatred my dad had toward me.

When I was nine years old, my stepfather had plans to sell me off for marriage. No one in the family knew of his plans, but as time went by he started acting and doing strange things that we all did not understand. He would come home with strange old men and ordered them to be well taken care of. After a short while my mother got the hint of his plan to get me married off to an old man. My mother could not stand the situation and she started looking for help to rescue me from being married off. No one was willing to help her except one of my uncles, who took her to the chief of our area. When she was still looking for help, my stepdad decided to marry me off at night when no one would see me go with the three old men. Fortunately, he never succeeded, because the children welfare officers were already aware of the incident and the police came to my rescue.

I was then taken to the Ngong police station where the division officer and Aunty Faith (a social worker for the north Kajiado area) were able to find a place where I could be safe and have my basic needs provided for. I was brought to Huruma Children's Home on the fourth of September, 2002, where I met a loving, kind-hearted mother who was willing to educate me and provide for my needs. I started my schooling here at Huruma and attended from nursery class all the way to Grade 8, where I did my primary final examination and did quite well. I was able to join the high school level from the year 2012 and am currently in the 10th grade, looking forward to joining the 11th grade in the coming year. I am very proud of my foster mum, who has brought me up in a Godly way that I will never forget. I remember where God has brought me from. Gladly, at the age of 18, I am given permission every holiday to pay a visit to my native place and spend time with my siblings.

My mother is now a divorcee who depends on her own strength and works tirelessly to educate my other siblings. My greatest obligation is to work extremely hard in school, get a good job in the future, and go back to my native place as a successful young lady. My ambition is to become one of the greatest lawyers or a great business woman in the nation of Kenya. Thank you to God for a great mother, Mama Zipporah, who has impacted my life positively.

Mirrium "Miracle" Njeri
I was born in 1999. My mother died because of AIDS. Many people never thought I would survive because I was infected. My aunt later brought us to Huruma in September 1999 because our relatives could not take care of us. Mama Zipporah Wanjiku, the founder of Huruma Children's Home, decided to take us because she knew my aunt. Mama Zipporah always hoped and prayed that God would heal me. God told her to feed me with a lot of carrots and have faith that I would get healed. I was six months old when I came to Huruma. In 2000, that's when God healed me, and everyone believed it was a miracle, including Mama Zipporah. That's the reason why Mama gave

me the name Miracle. I am now in grade six and I am not suffering from HIV anymore.

I give thanks to the Lord that I am now alive and living a better life. I thank Mama Zipporah because of her struggle to bring me up and the kids that live in Huruma up to today. My one brother finished his KCSE in 2013 and the other one will finish in 2014. I am trying to work hard and finish my KCPE and my KCSE so that I can see my dreams come true. I really thank God and owe Him a lot of gratitude for what He has done in my life and how far he has taken me. May God bless Mama Zipporah for her good and kind heart and may He continue to multiply the days of her life.

Helen Nyakiringa
I joined the Huruma Children's Home in 1990 after my mother passed away due to an unmentionable cause. Mama Zipporah took me and the rest of my family (three sisters and one brother) when we were under the care of my grandparents. Life was hard to stay with them so through the mercies of God Mama Zipporah came for our rescue before it was too late despite the many problems she herself had.

Though I was only four years old, I can partly remember how the home was. The house itself was made of blocks of mud that used to fall during the night. The rooms inside were divided with some tall branches of trees. The kitchen was small and located somewhere outside within the small compound. A dining hall was a kind of dream, we had never heard of such a thing so we never thought of it. We would stay outside as we waited for supper singing to our God. At times, food was a kind of history. Problems were many.

There is a story I can partly remember. There was a time in the early 1990s when the home was made up of less than 30 children and when a morsel of food was gold. We used to share the small portions among ourselves when it was available. There was a time when there was nothing to eat in the whole house. We went for seven days without taking anything except water. But after the seven days God provided food in a mighty way. During this time Mum used to spend sleepless nights praying and fasting and at all times crying. She never took a share of the food—it was more important that her children ate. Dad was a veterinarian by then, and working a lot of the time, so most of the times he was not around and it was Mum who took care of us.

The word Huruma means mercy to me because I know I've seen the mercies of God through Mum. She has been taking children of different cases out of mercy. Huruma means a lot to me. It is love and even how to care for others.

My favorite Bible verses are Jeremiah 29:11 and Psalms 27:10. Even if my mother and father desert me God will take care of me and God has good plans for me to give me a hope and a future. I know God has good plans for me which will prosper me after all the struggles I've gone through in life. After being one of the children from the home, my current position is a teacher. I enjoy interacting with kids and teachers. Those are good to live with as they make me always happy. I also enjoy teaching though it's not my profession. I am currently working to save money for my University education.

In the future I desire to be a nurse. I've observed and seen how people struggle out of sickness and it hurts me a lot. I feel like making the years go faster so as to reach that time for me to save the lives of those people who are struggling with curable diseases.

God has done and provided a lot for the home of which I can't tell all. From a muddy house, God built for us a big stony house and a cemented one. Out of the 30 children we were in early 1990s God has multiplied to 150+. Out of the very small land we had, God has expanded the boundaries to 6 acres. God has also given the home fame throughout the world, touching volunteers from everywhere to come and visit.

Now the home is in the process of building a multi-million shilling school and clinic and soon also dormitories are to be built.

I thank God for the much He has done for me and for the home at large. Out of the five members in our family, two have gone, and now I and my brother have been left. I look forward to being a HEROINE one day in the future.

Sammy Kariuki
To Mum Zipporah,
Dear Mum, I am very sorry of everything I have been doing to you that has made you angry with me. I am willing to change and make up my future bright. I am writing this letter telling you how hard it has been living outside the home for one month. It was such an experience for me entering in court of which I had never dreamt of. I will live as I have promised in juvenile court in Nairobi. I am very happy that you have taken me back home. Thank you for taking a step to help me. I know that I have a promising life of which I have to accomplish. There is a saying that an English man said that, "The will of God is the great sun toward which the soul must always keep facing as the sunflower faces the sun." That is why I am willing to change.

From,
Sammy Kariuki

✹✹✹✹✹✹✹

Sammy came to us as a street child. All we knew of Sammy's background was that he was born in 1989, he belonged to the Kikuyu tribe, he was an orphan, and he had no known next of kin. He spent much of his time living on the street, where he had no choice but to steal in order to survive.

As with many of the children we receive, it is hard for them to adjust to a new environment and remove themselves from their past tendencies. Upon arriving at Huruma, there have been two accounts of Sammy stealing from our home. In September of 2005, the Republic of Kenya's Children's Court issued a probation order against Sammy Kariuki for theft (unrelated to Huruma). Despite this, I did not give up on him and I continued to see great potential within him. I accepted Sammy back into the home, and I praise God, for he has made great efforts to improve himself. Sammy is now succeeding in his education and has remained true to his promise—since then he has not once brought harm to the Huruma Children's Home.

"So I will say with confidence, 'The Lord is my helper; I will not be afraid. What can man do to me?'"—Hebrews 13:6

Virginia

I'm Virginia. I was born in 1989, and I'm 17 years old. I was born in a place called Muranga in a small village called Kahuhia. That's where I was born, but when I was born my mother did not want a baby girl, so she threw me away. That's when my grandmother collected me and cared for me. I did not want to go and live with my grandmother, but I was a very small child, and at that time I could say nothing. So I agreed to stay with my grandmother. She took me with her when she left; she was going to search for a job. When I reached six years old, my mother went to the police and reported my grandmother, saying that my grandmother had taken me away from her. But that was a lie. But, because my grandmother loved her daughter, she just gave back me to my mother without quarreling. My mother and I stayed with my grandmother for one year.

Then, one day, my mother got sick and had to lie down on the bed. She told me to cook lunch for her, and when the food was ready I woke her up and told her to eat. She woke up and ate a little of the food and went back to sleep again. She told me to save the rest, because she was going to eat it later. I left the house and closed our door and I went to play outside our house. I later went back to the house and tried to wake her up again, but this time was different, because she never woke up. I called and called, but she never answered. That's when I called my neighbor to help me. My neighbor came and she lifted my mother's hand then let it fall down. When I saw this, I told my neighbor to leave her, and that she would wake up later. I did not know that she was dead.

That was when I ran away from my home and went to live on the streets alone, and left my mother dead on the bed. When I was on the streets, the police came at night and took all the street children, including me, to jail. We were asked questions like, "Why are you on the street?" one by one. When it was my turn, I said that my mother is dead on the bed and there is no one to help me. That's when the police took a car and we left to go to my home that night. When we reached my home, we found that my mother was still on the bed. We took everything that my mother owned from the house and we brought my mother to the mortuary center. The next day we went and buried my mother. The most amazing thing is that I never cried, because I did not know what was happening. I was just seven years old. When we finished the burial, my grandmother and I went away together.

But the things that belonged to my mother were never given to my grandmother. In fact, my grandmother owned nothing. So we had nowhere to stay. We went to search for somewhere to work in a *shamba* (vegetable garden). My grandmother was trying to find work that would pay and give us somewhere to sleep, because we did not have a house that we could call our own. We had no aunt or uncle who could help us. We had nobody in the front or at the side, neither at the back. We had no one to help us, so we got use to migrating at all times of the day.

One day, we were searching for a job and went to see a woman who owned a plot of houses. The woman gave us a house that we could live in and it became our house forever. My grandmother used to work on that woman's shamba and I used to play outside with other children. But one day I was very hungry, and we had nothing to eat. I went to another shamba and stole sugarcane. Because I did not know how to run fast, I was grabbed by the owner of the shamba. He took me to his house and told me that this was my end of living. I could not believe him, so I cried so much, saying that I'm alone in my family with only my grandmother. I begged for him to release me, saying that I was sorry, and that I would not steal again. But he did not listen to me. He had me convinced that he was going to kill me. I cried louder and louder. But no one had any mercy on me.

The man asked me whether my grandmother was very old, and I said yes. He told me that because of my grandmother, he was not going to kill me. I swallowed a gulp of saliva, feeling very happy. Later they released me, minus my sugarcane. When my grandmother came back from work she found out what had happened, and she quarreled and beat me so much. I was very sad, and I told her that I was stealing because I was not going to school. That's when the woman who had given us a place to stay told my grandmother that there is a place where she could take me so that I can be busy and would not steal.

I was taken to be approved by the home's manager. I stayed there for two months before I was taken to Huruma Children's Home. Huruma is now my home and I hope that it will make a difference in me, and I pray I will be able to stay in Huruma all the days of my life until I get married. I'm sure it will happen. In Jesus' name.

The verse that I like in the Bible is Matthew 5:44–45: "Love your enemies and pray for those who persecute you that you may be sons of your Father in heaven." The reason why I like this verse is because it talks about loving those who hurt you and that you should love even your enemies.

Isaiah Amondi

My name is Isaiah Amondi. I am only 13 years old, but my background is bad. At first, I was living with my parents, brothers, and sisters. Our home was in the northeastern part of Kenya. At that time it was like hell. My mother caught the disease called TB (tuberculosis) and she had to stay in the hospital for six months. All the while my father was getting thinner and thinner. He was taken to the hospital by my mum and my uncle, but they couldn't help him. It was a hard time for me, and for my father, things were getting very ugly. My father was taken to where his mum was living. He stayed for two weeks and three days. My father died on Thursday, April 25, in 2005. My uncles came and demanded from my mum all of our property, including my father's welding machine. The only thing which my mum could do was cry. Because of what my uncles had done, we were left with nothing. On Saturday, my father was buried, and we slept there the following day. My mum and my brothers and sisters came to Kajiado, the place where my grandmother was living. But my mother didn't stay for long; she stayed for half a year and then died. My grandmother could not afford to feed us because she was already paying for our schooling. We would wake up and go to school hungry. After school we could wait for the food the school gave out. It was only boiled *maize* (a tough corn) but it was at least something to eat. Meanwhile, my grandmother was finding for us a boarding school. She found for us the Huruma Children's Home in Ngong. Before we came to live at the Home, we were checked over by the doctors to see if we were sick. We found that everyone in my family, except my sister Mercy, had HIV. When I heard that I had HIV I couldn't believe it. It was very hard to hear that I had HIV. But me, I believe in the Bible. And although Mum usually said that I hate God, and that that was why I was sick, I knew that was a lie.

After staying at Huruma for some time, I was checked again by the doctor, who found that there was no disease in my body. "PRAISE BE TO THE LORD!" I said. I have been healed and don't have HIV. I am very thankful.

When I am grown, I want to be a pilot.

Jecinat Kavinya

I am Jecintah Kavinya Kithome. The main reason as to why I came to Huruma Children's Home is that I was very sick, with a very big wound on my left leg, and my parents did not want to take me to the hospital because their religion did not believe in taking people to hospitals or taking any kind of medication. I was rescued by some of the villagers who lived within our village, my grandmother among them, who took me to the hospital for my leg to be treated. I was very ill; I thought that I was not going to get well. While in the hospital, my parents never came to visit me.

The only people who came to visit me were the church members. Several months later I was well and needed to go back to school, but the children's department was reluctant to take me home. When I insisted, they took me to Huruma Children's Home. I was placed one class behind, because I was a little bit behind.

Huruma Children's Home has changed my life completely. I am in Grade 7, going to Grade 8, and am doing very well in my education. I have seen the hand of God leading me. I came to Huruma Children's Home in 2006 and I stayed in Huruma for four years without visiting my family members. None of them even knew where I was; some of them thought I was dead. But a time came when I had to go back home. Everyone was shocked to see me. It was very hard for me to live with them, but I had to forgive them because, east or west, home is best.

Rehema Saitoti
My parents abandoned me and my brothers and the police brought us to Huruma. It was in December 1992 when it was still made of mud. I was 6 and came with my two little brothers. I did not speak their Kikuyu language because I was from a Masai tribe. It was hard because I did not understand what was going on. I had to learn their Kikuyu language quickly.

I grew up in the home. When I was 19, I took Huruma for granted and ran away. All I had with me was my clothes. I quickly learned that life on my own was hard. I wanted to come back but I couldn't. Life was very hard and I was not happy. I did not know anyone and I had nowhere to go.

In March 2005, I went back to Mum. Huruma was still home to me and I wanted to go back. I had been working as a house-maid but I decided to use everything I earned to come back and help Mum. I am thankful I was accepted back into Huruma. It

FINAL WORD:
THANK YOU FOR YOUR SUPPORT

T HE CHILDREN OF the Huruma Children's Home wish to thank you for your support. All proceeds raised by the sale of *Mother to the Motherless* have gone directly to meet their needs. Funds generated are furthering the education of the children, providing them with proper nutrition and clothing, as well as much needed medical supplies and attention. Simply by purchasing this book, you have helped improve their standard of life. Thank you. For further information on how you can support our ministry or how you can sponsor a child, please visit our website at: www.hurumachildrenshome.org

While sponsorship is improving the lives of abandoned children, the most essential support you can offer is through prayer. Our humble request is that you please pray for God's continued provision as the Lord proceeds to use us to meet the needs of His children; for He is a Father to the fatherless (Psalm 68:5). If you are interested in becoming a Huruma prayer partner, monthly updates are available through our website. Thank you, and may God bless you for your support.

With much love in Christ,

> Mama Zipporah
> Executive Director
> Huruma Children's Home